HOW TO
SING

HOW TO SING

Graham Hewitt

Illustrated by
Shirley Bellwood

Elm Tree Books
EMI Music Publishing

To Rebecca, Joe, Mary and Sally

First published in Great Britain 1978
by Elm Tree Books Ltd
90 Great Russell Street, London WC1B 3PT

in association with

EMI Music Publishing Ltd
138–140 Charing Cross Road, London WC2H 0LD

British Library Cataloguing in Publication Data
Hewitt, Graham
    How to sing.
    1. Singing
    I. Title
    784.9   MT893

ISBN 0 241 89897 8 hardback
          0 241 89915 X paperback

Music examples processed by CMPS, Cambridge
Design and production in association with Book Production Consultants.
Printed in Great Britain at The Burlington Press.

CONTENTS

INTRODUCTION

Not long ago, a friend of mine was telling me about his search to find a good singing teacher. He had tried several — some of them expensive — during the past few years, but none of them had 'understood' his voice, with the result that he was confused about 'the correct way to sing' and making little or no improvement.

My own early experience was very similar. For fifteen years I had tried as many different teachers, some for long periods, and although my studies weren't a complete waste of time, everything I learned could have been acquired from a few dozen lessons and without the gobbledegook I experienced along the way.

Reading about singing is probably less helpful. Of the books I have been able to find and read, again only a few have helped and many have left me unsure about what to do to improve my singing.

All the available books contain scholarly observations about the biology of vocal organs, acoustics and psychiatry — fine for mathematicians or doctors, but few contain any simple and clear instructions to help the *singer*.

No book, or teacher for that matter, can transform average talent into a Caruso or a Barbra Streisand: 'star quality' and musical sensitivity cannot be taught. There are, however, some fundamental truths about singing, most of them easy to understand, which can help to improve and develop your present singing ability; and this book tries to clarify and condense the helpful information into a form which anyone can understand.

Whether you sing, or would like to sing, pop music, early folk music, madrigals or revue; whether you belong to a church choir, a rock group, a barber-shop quartet or an operatic society, as a beginner, an amateur or a professional, of any age, *using* this handbook will help you to recognise what good singing is, to eliminate your faults and to develop the vocal strengths you already possess.

As it is written for everybody who sings, there may be a few pages which are not relevant to some styles of singing. But somewhere in the book, you will find information which concerns *your* voice and *your type* of singing.

If you give it a try, your singing will improve — you will notice the difference in a few weeks.

GRAHAM HEWITT

CHAPTER ONE

SUPER BREATHING:
FOR SINGING AND FOR HEALTH

Most writers and teachers of singing place a great deal of emphasis — and rightly, I think — on the importance of a study of breathing and breath control early on in the course of learning to sing. As long ago as the seventeenth century, the famous Italian teachers are known to have checked their pupils' breathing, firmly believing that 'he who breathes well, sings well'.

A well-developed technique of *controlled* breathing in and out is invaluable for singers and marvellous for anyone's general health. It will expand your chest an inch or two, flatten sagging tummy muscles and correct your posture. It also cleanses the lungs, re-oxygenates the blood efficiently and relaxes you when you are nervous or tense.

There are three aspects of breathing which the singer must acquire:

(1) The ability to inhale large quantities of air,

(2) The ability to snatch a good breath quickly,

(3) And, more important, the ability to control the escape of breath.

Breathing and breath control are two different studies, so I shall treat them separately, and, in this short chapter, talk about the simple study of deep breathing.

Deep, or Super Breathing

The volume of air needed to keep the body 'ticking-over' when you are relaxing listening to music, or reading a book, is small. Only the upper part of the lungs is used and the highest part of the chest moves up and down slightly. Just enough air to keep you going is taken in — the breathing is 'shallow'.

As the singer needs to sustain long phrases, sometimes for fifteen or twenty seconds, he obviously needs considerable reserves of breath, and this can be taken in only by using *all* the capacity of the lungs.

It is important to remember that to give the lungs a good spring-clean, you must empty them completely (to get rid of stale and stagnant air) as well as fill them. *Maximum* intake and *maximum* expulsion of breath must be developed, and this can be easily learned with a little patience and a few aches and pains from the muscles you haven't used before.

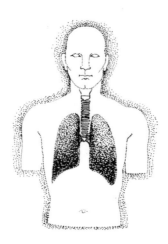

The lungs are pear-shaped — wider at the bottom than at the top. Everyone uses the narrow, upper sections, but the broad parts at the bottom are rarely exercised. To fill them completely, you have to concentrate on the base of the lungs — not the upper chest. *The shoulders shouldn't move.*

Try this exercise to begin with:

Standing, with the fingers of both hands pressed into your sides at waist-level, slowly and easily take a deep breath, concentrating on filling-up from the bottom of the lungs. (You may find that breathing through the nose makes for a fuller, deeper breath, and, of course, it warms and cleans the air, making it less harsh on the throat.) Think of it as an extension of ordinary breathing: 'feel' the air going down, deep into the bottom part of your lungs.

If you are doing it properly, your hands will be eased out. This is because the lungs should expand downwards as well as sideways, and, in doing so, the muscles underneath are flattened and pushed outwards. By the way, if you have recently eaten a large meal, your full stomach will prevent these muscles from moving freely, and you will not be able to expand easily but experience a sensation of tightness.

If you are not used to doing this kind of breathing, you may not be able to expand fully at first. No one I have known has been able to breathe deeply at the first attempt, and women seem to find it more difficult than men. But with patience and steady practice it will come right. You will eventually 'sense' the correct way to do it and you will feel and see the increased expansion.

Here are a few more exercises to help you.

Try lying on your back to practise breathing exercises. When you are lying down, the breathing is deeper and you can easily feel the movement of the muscles.

Another thing which helps is to hold a heavy object above your head: use something heavy enough to make lifting it an effort — a bucket of sand or a bar-bell. Your breathing should fall easily into the right place.

Bear in mind that the expansion of the lungs and rib-cage is not only at the front of the body — the *whole* of the chest from the waist up also moves outwards at the back and the sides.

Here is an exercise which I find very helpful — it emphasises this all-round expansion. When you are doing it, think of how a balloon expands in all directions.

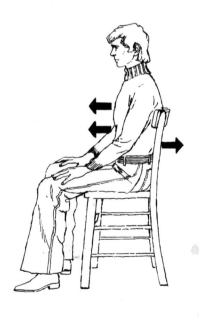 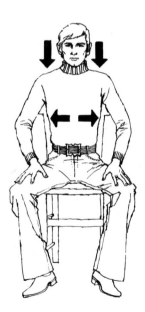

Sit on a firm, straight-backed chair, hang your arms loosely and move the elbows away from the sides of the chest. Without moving the shoulders and with your back touching the chair-back, take a long, slow, deep breath from the bottom of the lungs. Try to expand so that your back swells and presses against the chair. This exercise should quickly establish the sensation of waist and back expansion while breathing in.

So much for maximum *intake* of breath.

Super breathing also involves the maximum *outlet* of breath, and this is where the pains begin!

As you know, completely emptying the lungs gets rid of the stale air in the bottom of the lungs, and makes way for the new, clean air to re-oxygenate the entire lung tissue. Strictly speaking, this comes under the heading of lung health, and not in the study of singing (as one never sings to the point of exhaustion of breath). However, the muscles involved in maximum exhalation are also used in breath control, and it is for this reason that we should look at breath output for a while.

Standing up and having taken a full breath, begin *slowly* to blow out the breath. When your lungs are about half empty, your rib-cage will probably start to collapse; subconsciously you will assume that your lungs are empty and you will automatically take another breath. Your lungs will not be completely emptied, however, and a considerable amount of air will still be inside, so you will need to squeeze a bit more to complete the spring-clean!

Two skills have to be developed. First, holding the rib-cage as expanded as possible while breathing out, and second, pulling-in the abdominal muscles in order to exert a gentle upward pressure on the lungs from underneath. This will give a 'support' to the lungs as they are being emptied of the remaining air.

The expanded rib-cage is necessary for two reasons. 1. If you allow the chest to collapse, the outflow of breath may be too sudden for the *controlled* breathing out (which we shall look at in the next chapter). 2. The expanded chest position facilitates the quick snatch-breath which is sometimes necessary in a short rest between two long phrases. If you have allowed the chest to collapse towards the end of a long phrase, it will take a second or two and noticeable physical effort to expand it again, take a breath and start to sing. But if your rib-cage is *always* well-expanded, the snatch-breath can be taken simply by letting the air in — a quick process, sometimes necessary when you have only a crotchet or a quaver rest in which to fill up.

Now try the last exercise again — this time consciously keeping the chest fully expanded throughout. Your rib-cage will begin to deflate, so carry the chest high and *will* it to stay there whilst you gradually expel the air. When you are getting towards the end of the exercise, steadily pull in the muscles just below the navel, and continue to blow out smoothly and confidently. You should be able to continue this *steady* expiry of breath for several seconds longer than you thought possible, and although it might hurt at first, your abdominal muscles will develop flexibility and you will be able to support the lungs easily within a few weeks.

To make this deep in-and-out breathing more palatable, I would like to mention a further exercise. This one will get you out on the road, and so offers a little variety to the fairly uninteresting exercises described so far. Again, it will develop not only deep in-and-out breathing, but will also enable you to control the smooth outflow of breath which is vital to sustained singing.

Walk rhythmically at a steady pace and *gradually* inhale through the nose, counting how many steps you take, until the lungs are completely full (remember to fill from the base, keeping the shoulders down and the chest high and wide). Hold the breath for a few steps, in order to give the fresh air a chance to get to the tiny lung tissues, then slowly blow out through the mouth to a measured number of steps, keeping the chest high and drawing in the tummy muscles to squeeze out all the air. Repeat this several times.

I find this a marvellously bracing exercise. It cleanses the lungs and exercises the abdominal and chest muscles. Start by breathing in to five steps, pausing for five, and out to ten (you will probably find it takes almost twice as long to blow out the air as it does to take it in). Over a period, increase the number of steps to ten for breathing in, pause for ten, and out to twenty.

Here is a simple chart of progress on this exercise over a period of, say, one month. Devise your own charts for the other breathing exercises.

Day	1	2	3	4	5	6	7	8	9	10	11	12	13	14	15	16	17	18	19	20	21	22	23	24	25
Breathing in	5																								
Pause	5																								
Breathing out	10																								

CHAPTER TWO

BREATH CONTROL — OR CONTROL OF THE ESCAPING BREATH

How to Develop an Impressive Breath Control

You should now understand enough about healthy breathing to give you a sufficiently large breath capacity for whatever type of singing you do.

Next — and perhaps even more important — is to know how to control the outflow of breath when you are singing. Breath control has to be developed for two reasons:

1. Composers sometimes write long phrases of music for the singer to cope with, and, unless the singer knows how to budget the outgoing supply of air, he is going to run out of it quickly and be forced to break a long phrase which should be sung in one breath.

2. When you are singing a fairly long phrase, the pressure which forces the air to escape through the vocal cords *must be sustained*, otherwise your voice will sound as though you are running out of breath. It will sound weak or 'pale', and may have a 'wobble'.

At any point during singing a sustained phrase, you *must* be using the minimum amount of breath necessary and you must also support the pressure of its escape.

As a matter of interest, and to help you to understand what happens during breathing in and out, here is a simple description of respiration.

The lungs are encased by the ribs. Underneath the lungs is the diaphragm, a dome-shaped muscle — rather like half a grapefruit, but much bigger — which forms a kind of floor to the lungs and divides the chest from the tummy area. As you breathe in, the lungs and ribs expand, the diaphragm is flattened and pushed downwards, and the abdominal muscles are pressed down and out. In breathing out the abdominal muscles and the diaphragm soon return to their original

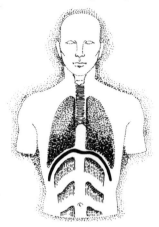

positions, the rib-cage contracts back to its original position, and between them they squeeze out most of the air.

The direction of the movement when breathing in is outwards and downwards and the direction of movement when breathing out is inwards and upwards. Like this:

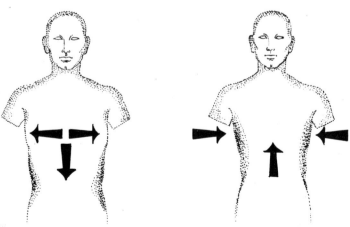

The ribs and the diaphragm will not stay in the expanded position for long. Their natural elasticity will quickly return them to the position of rest. When this happens, there is a rush of breath, as in a sigh, too much air escapes for comfortable singing and within a few seconds it has all gone. Just what the singer does *not* want to happen.

What we have to do, therefore, is to *prevent* the chest and the diaphragm from their usual quick return to their relaxed position, so that *we* control the amount of air escaping. The *singer* must determine how much air he will use, and how long it will last him. He *rations* the supply.

Compare this process with holding an inflated balloon. Your index finger and thumb correspond to your vocal cords — a sort of 'valve' — and the balloon represents your lungs. If your finger pressure is just right, the air will escape at a steady rate, but without help from you the balloon will expire itself quickly. This is similar to what happens when singing.

<u>Breath control</u>, then, is about two things: *controlling* <u>the escape of air, and</u> <u>supporting</u> its pressure of escape.

Let's look at an exercise which will develop this control of escaping air. In this exercise, try to keep the chest well expanded while letting the air escape: you will not, of course, be able to keep it *rigid* — it will reduce in size *a little*, but *don't let it collapse*. At the same time, don't allow the diaphragm to spring back. Try to keep the chest wide, and the diaphragm should behave itself. This time, don't *blow* out the air — vocal sound should not be *forced* out, it escapes gradually from the vocal-cord 'valve' — but sing a low note quietly or expire on the letter F with your top teeth on the lower lip.

Here is the <u>exercise</u>: Stand relaxed and take a breath (from the bottom of your lungs, of course) — the shoulders should be hanging loose as if you were carrying two buckets of water. Now expire on F or a low note, slowly, gradually and evenly — don't collapse the chest, even at the end of the breath, imagine you are expanding it and this will ensure it stays high. It will pull on the abdonimal muscles and hurt until you are used to it.

Don't continue until you are exhausted, but towards the end take another breath and repeat the exercise.

If your stomach muscles are out of condition, you will find some difficulty in performing this exercise smoothly. You can improve their flexibility and strength with any of the well-known stomach muscle exercises such as 'sit-ups' from a lying-down position. Another good exercise, also from a lying-down position, is to raise the ankles slowly an inch or two from the ground.

And now a little about the second reason for breath control: *to support and sustain the pressure of its escape*.

Back to the balloon again. It is well-inflated, and your fingers are allowing air to escape at a steady rate, which will empty the balloon in about twenty seconds. The rate of escape will remain fairly constant for a few seconds, and the high-pitched note it makes will remain 'in pitch'. Only for three or four seconds though: thereafter the air pressure inside the balloon falls, the rate at which the air escapes slows down and the note it makes drops in pitch. However, if you support the base of the balloon with your other hand and ease the air out, the pressure of its escape can remain constant throughout and the note will not *sag*.

Something similar happens in singing.

Almost as soon as you start to sing a long phrase, the diaphragm should *gradually*, not suddenly, raise itself to give support underneath the lungs. This keeps constant the pressure of escaping air, and *must* be continued until you have finished singing. By about the middle of the long phrase, you may feel that you are running out of breath, but you are not. There is plenty of air still in the lungs and there is a way of making it work for you to give the voice a new lease of life.

The support given to the lungs by the upward movement of the diaphragm can be reinforced by pulling-in the abdominal muscles below the diaphragm. By doing so, you can guarantee a strong and steady vocal sound right up to the end of the longest phrase. This pulling-in of the abdomen also happens when you cough, but the best way to feel it is by blowing up the balloon again!

A new balloon is stiff: you need a lot of puff, more pressure, to stretch the rubber. Your cheeks are blown up, but nothing happens until you automatically pull in the muscles just below your waist. This extra 'kick' which the breath gets produces enough pressure to inflate the balloon. It is exactly what should happen when you are sustaining your singing — and so I hope you have a few balloons handy!

That is all there is to breath control. It is awkward to describe, but easy to do. Re-read what I've written and feel your breathing movements until you think you understand. Then try this simple exercise.

The object is to sing a note and hold it steady for as long as is comfortable. Use only a small amount of breath, control the escape of it, and support the note to give it some 'life'. Choose a pitch you can hold easily, say B♭ for low voices and E♭ for high voices, and, if you find it easier at first, hum instead of sing. Whilst you are doing this little exercise, be aware of the muscle movements we have just talked about, and sing with confidence — knowing that you can sustain this line of sound for as long as you wish.

Here is another — and this is probably the most valuable of all breath control exercises. It is called the 'messa di voce' — the Italian term for starting a note quietly, increasing its volume until it is loud and gradually decreasing back to almost nothing. It is written like this —

— 'hairpins' to some musicians. Choose a comfortable pitch in the middle of your range, sing on OO , AH , a hum or anything you find easy, make the rise and fall in volume slow and gradual, 'play' with your voice, feel that you have control over it and repeat the messa di voce twice if you have enough breath.

Finally, here is another exercise which will quickly show you how much air should be escaping. Sing in front of a lighted candle without making the flame flicker. As we have said earlier, singers don't *blow out* the breath, it is under pressure only as far as the vocal cords. Thereafter, it disperses and escapes through the mouth. It is not *forced* out of the mouth, then, and so the flame should not move if you are singing properly.

Hold the candle about nine inches from your face, sing a phrase or an exercise easily, gently, with proper breath support and crescendo if you wish. The flame should barely move. It's a very old exercise, but a valuable one, I think.

Make up some exercises yourself and record your development by timing your performance in seconds and devising a chart or graph.

SUMMARY/NOTES

CHAPTER THREE
POSTURE — OR BODY SHAPE

Before we move on to the vocal exercise in the next chapter, I would like to mention a few points about the most suitable posture for singing.

As you already know, there is a great deal of muscle movement going on inside you during singing. If your posture prevents these organs and muscles from moving freely, your singing will be affected.

The part of the body involved is from the bottom of the spine to the back of the head. This area is not upright, in a straight line, even when you are standing. There are three curves in it: one at the hips, one in the middle of your back, and the third is your neck. Stand against a wall and notice the spaces behind your neck and at the bottom of your back. These curves have to be straightened, so that the body is as upright as you can make it (not in a dead-straight line, that is impossible, but as straight as is *comfortable*).

Stand against a wall with your heels about six inches apart and your feet in a V-shape, and I will take you through the adjustments which have to be made. First, do a go-go dancer's swivel of the hips to press the bottom of your back against the wall. This will straighten the lowest curve. Then, tuck in the chin and ease your back and neck towards the wall to straighten the other curves. Without changing this upright position, ease yourself a few inches away from the wall and transfer your balance from the heels to the balls of your feet. Relax a little so that you feel *poised*, not rigid, and this is the best position for singing.

From your waist up, feel that you have stretched an inch or two. Feel the 'walk-tall' sensation which models have when they balance books on their heads. To keep the shoulders down, imagine you are carrying two heavy shopping baskets.

You should feel alert, balanced, poised and ready for action — like the high-diver's stance at the moment when he springs from the board. Experiment with this posture until you feel it is right: it will improve your appearance as well as your singing.

If you have to sing while you are sitting — as guitarists, keyboard players and opera singers sometimes do — try to preserve this body-shape so that you don't slouch.

The amout of space in your mouth is another factor which influences the sound of your voice.

There are two jaw positions: the 'chewing' position and the 'biting' position. To feel the difference, place your fingers close to your ear while you chew. There is very little movement. But when you bite, the lower jaw is displaced from its socket near the ear, and drops to create more space between the back teeth. This is the position for singing. The increased space in the mouth helps to 'amplify' the sound of your voice.

(There are a few occasions when this shape is not possible: the vowel EE on a low pitch is one of them. But, generally speaking, the more space the better.)

CHAPTER FOUR

ATTACK AND ENDING THE NOTE

The way you start a note is, in my opinion, as important as any other aspect of vocal technique. When I say 'the way you start a note', I mean your entire technique of starting, including all the physical movements you make at the time the vocal cords vibrate and produce the sound. The 'attack' involves not only the vocal cords, but also the position of the tongue and throat, the amount of space in the mouth and the breath pressure. All these factors influence and determine the sound of your voice *at the moment of attack*, and altering the position of any one of them will alter the sound you make. The attack, then, sets the seal for your 'fundamental sound' — it is *vital* to your singing.

Suppose, for instance, that the basic sound you make is, say, 'throaty' — building up the volume will produce a loud, throaty sound. If it is 'breathy' — by developing vocal agility you will have a flexible voice which sounds breathy. And, if your voice is raucous, extending your range will result in a voice capable of singing high and low, but which sounds awful!

Once the attack is right, however, the sound will be right, and you can *then* begin to develop your voice. To try to develop it *before* the start of the note is correct is a waste of time.

If you have ever stood outside practice studios while some singing lessons are being given, you will know what I mean. I have heard the same vocal exercises week after week. The unfortunate pupil is made to sing higher, louder, and faster than in the previous lesson, but his *real technique* of singing is ignored. Practising like this will disappoint the singer, because he will not make any noticeable improvement.

So the attack — the start of the note — is all-important, and we will look at it now.

Imagine you are about to start to sing this well-known song — or any other phrase which starts with a vowel, for that matter. This is what happens.

You have taken a breath, and your posture, of course, is right. You imagine (mentally 'hear') the pitch of the first note. Your mouth opens a little, the tongue lies flat out of the way, the vocal cords are vibrated by a small amount of breath pressure, and the sound of 'If' is made. (Several thought processes and movements take place — but it all happens in a split-second.) That is what should happen. Do you start the note like this? Have a go and try to 'feel' the movements.

The way you attack a note is by now second-nature to you: you have developed the technique over the years and it has become automatic. But it may not be as good as it could be. Lots of factors can affect it: the position of the tongue is one, and how wide your mouth is open is another.

These are some of the things we should look at: mental 'hearing' of the sound, vocal cord action, minimum breath, enough mouth space and tongue position. We will talk about these points and make up some exercises which will establish a good start to the note and correct any faults. If you practise them properly, you will eventually make a good attack without even thinking about it.

Mentally 'Hearing' the Sound

If you start to sing without concentrating on the first note, you might find that the start of the note is a little shaky. You could be 'off the note' and the vowel sound might not be pure. In the few bars of piano introduction, *imagine* the exact pitch of the first note — 'hear' it in your mind and hear a beautiful vowel sound. Imagine the *exact* sound you want to make — and you will make it! I don't know what happens — perhaps imagining the sound positions the vocal cords correctly — but I can promise you it works. Try it and see!

Vocal Cord Action

The vocal cords are set in the *larynx* (the voice box or 'Adam's apple'). They are tiny folds of skin, attached either side of the windpipe. Think of them as window shutters. During breathing, they open to allow the air to pass in and out, but when you prepare to sing, the shutters close leaving just a 'chink' of light between them. The pressure of the column of air underneath the cords sets them vibrating and a sound is made. This sound is amplified by the spaces in the throat, and it escapes through the mouth.

The larynx mechanism is very delicate and can be easily damaged by harsh treatment. The word *attack* is not suitable to describe its action. An aggressive start to the note is very bad news. The start of the note should be smooth and gentle — *caress* is a better word than *attack*. One teacher likens the start of the note to letting-in the clutch of a car — there shouldn't be a jerk or a shock, but a smooth movement. We can show it in a diagram:

The sound shouldn't suddenly 'explode', you shouldn't 'bang' the note like this:

The start must always be gradual:

You can jerk the attack by being too earnest, too stiff: make it easy, relaxed, 'stroke' the start of the note — a gentle movement.

Here is a helpful sensation: Say A EGG slowly, making a short break between the A and the E. The E of Egg needs a separate attack and there is a definite 'click' when the larynx opens and the air escapes. This 'click' starts the note, and it has to be a gentle 'stroking' movement. *Attacking it aggressively can damage your cords and ruin your voice.*

Try to make a 'clean' start to each note. Open your mouth comfortably wide, keep your tongue flat, and use the minimum of breath necessary. Don't sing HAH-HAH-, this will make a 'breathy' sound.

Modify the exercise to suit your own voice: transpose it into a low and comfortable pitch if you wish, or use a vowel sound which you find easy. Remember: easy, relaxed, almost nonchalant — don't be too keen!

Here is another simple exercise — in the Bass Clef and a minor key this time —

Slow

EE AH EE AH EE AH EE AH EE AH EE AH EE AH

Again, use any vowels you wish (consonants come later). Work at first in the middle part of your voice and gradually, over a period of weeks or months, extend the exercises to include all the *comfortable* notes in your range.

Make a new 'click' on every note: start each note separately and deliberately.

Always use only a minimum of breath — don't *push* the air out, don't 'cough' the sound out. You might remember: minimum breath, but maximum mouth space.

At least maximum *comfortable* space. If the mouth is tight and stiff, the sound will be tight and stiff. Open the mouth and throat fairly wide — don't stretch it — it should be comfortably wide for the vowel and the note you are singing.

Tongue and Throat

Your tongue is much bigger than it appears to be! It goes a long way back into the throat, and its muscles are joined to the voice box. If you touch your 'Adam's apple' while you move your tongue forward and backward, you will see what I mean. It follows, then, that if your tongue is too far forward or, more commonly, going back, it can interfere with the larynx, affecting its free movement and changing the sound of your voice. If it is too far back, it will also constrict the throat space.

The best position for the tongue is lying relaxed on the floor of the mouth, with its tip resting against the back of the teeth. One of my teachers said that it should be flat in the mouth like the first layer of pastry pressed into the bottom of a baking tray.

The worst position is for it to be pulled up and back into the throat. Some men tend to do this when they are trying to make a deep, resonant, manly sound! This position will choke the throat and produce a constricted sound.

Only a few singers have a serious problem with the tongue. If you are not one of them — and you probably aren't — forget it! Too much worrying about it will quickly turn you into a hypochondriac, and then the tongue *will* be unruly.

If you feel that your tongue does move back and narrow the throat space, practise rubbing the tip of the tongue on the back of the teeth. This will establish a comfortable position, and over a period of weeks your tongue should lie flat.

Another trick which helps is to hold the tip with a handkerchief while you sing some easy phrases or vowels.

The throat and jaw should be easy, relaxed, and 'natural'. There should not be any aches, stiffness, or soreness in them. If there is, and you are uncomfortable, it is wrong, and you are not singing properly. Correct it by moving the jaw from side to side to loosen it, assume a 'yawning' position to relax the throat and experiment with the exercises in this section until you sing comfortably.

The vowels ER and OO are especially useful in loosening up any tightness. In singing these vowels, the throat, tongue and jaw seem to fall into a relaxed position. The consonant K does the same thing. So if you practise on KER and KOO, you should begin to produce a relaxed and comfortable attack.

Here is one exercise to start you off —

Slow

KER KER KER KER   KER KER KER   KOO KOO KOO KOO   KOO KOO KOO

Compose a few more exercises on starting the note, suitable for your own voice.

These eight exercises, which will guide you when composing some yourself, should be used for your own voice in different keys and using other vowels as you wish. Don't forget: easy, gentle, clean, relaxed — no bashing! You'll soon hear an improvement in the clarity of your attack.

Slowly

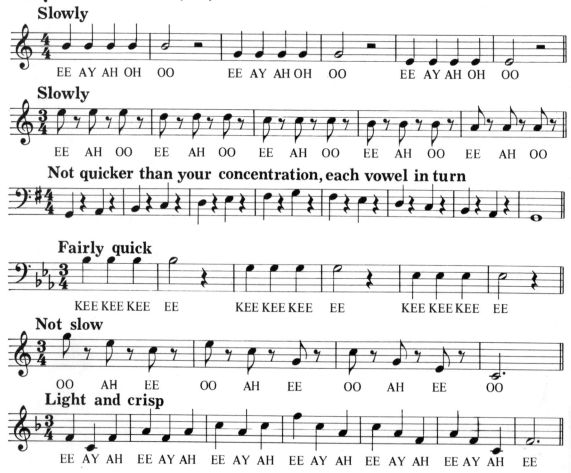

EE AY AH OH   OO   EE AY AH OH   OO   EE AY AH OH   OO

Slowly

EE   AH   OO   EE   AH   OO   EE   AH   OO   EE   AH   OO   EE   AH   OO

Not quicker than your concentration, each vowel in turn

Fairly quick

KEE KEE KEE   EE   KEE KEE KEE   EE   KEE KEE KEE   EE

Not slow

OO   AH   EE   OO   AH   EE   OO   AH   EE   OO

Light and crisp

EE AY AH   EE AY AH   EE AY AH   EE AY AH   EE AY AH   EE AY AH   EE

Gentle, easy

EE EE EE EE EE   EE   AY AY AY AY AY   AY   AH AH AH AH AH etc.

Leisurely

K K K K KER ER ER ER   ER   K K K K KOO OO OO OO   OO

Here is some space for notes, and a page of manuscript paper.

NOTES

Ending the Sound

The way that a note is finished can sometimes spoil what would otherwise have been a well-sung line.

Look at this line of a song for example:

The music is written in *phrases*, not one note at a time. A musical phrase can be likened to a phrase or a clause of words — and it should be performed as one line of sound, not as several individual notes. In the example, 'May each day in the week be a good day' is one phrase and the second 'May' begins a new line. A small breath is taken after 'good day', whether you need it or not, in order to punctuate the music. A 'comma' in the 'sentence of music', so to speak.

The composer indicates the phrasing he wants by drawing a phrase mark, a long, curved line, over the notes in the phrase. This phrase mark is a good visual reminder to sing the notes in a long, smooth, unbroken line of sound.

If you were singing the first phrase, you probably wouldn't want to sing it all at the same volume. You would, perhaps, start quietly, build towards 'good', and ease off at the end of the phrase to make it a musically satisfying line of sound. Whatever volume you are singing at when you get to 'good', you will have to gradually taper it off to nothing if you want to make a smooth end to the phrase. If you sing 'day' at the *same* volume throughout, the end of the phrase will be sudden

and abrupt — like this: | day | instead of like this: day ▷

So the sound should gradually die away until it stops naturally. This is the way to end a note and you should aim to finish all phrases similarly (with the obvious exception of those which have to be spat out for a dramatic effect).

When you are singing in duet or in trio, it is even more important for voices to 'phrase-off' like this, otherwise one singer will predominate and the 'blend' or balance will be spoilt.

Here's another example:

During this passage from Bach's 'B Minor Mass', the alto soloist has to sing slower and quieter, and she normally makes a long pause on the last note, until it gradually dies away. This technique of ending the note gradually isn't easy, and so you will have to practise carefully if you want to do it perfectly. It is done by continuously reducing the breath pressure until the sound eventually stops — almost unnoticed.

Here are two exercises to develop the technique:

Treat each pair of notes as the end of a phrase — make a short break at the commas — fade-out the sound on the second note of the pair until it 'disappears into thin air'.

Your voice might be a bit shaky as it becomes quieter. If it is, this is probably because you are timid at first and perhaps not using *enough* breath. Sing confidently and more strongly and you will find the gradual decrease of breath easier to control.

Again, the same procedure as in the previous exercise.

These upward-moving phrase-ends are more difficult to sing and this often produces a flat note unless you are pitch conscious.

On this manuscript paper, make up some similar exercises specifically for your voice. Use all vowels, throughout your range, and also include phrases from music in your repertoire.

CHAPTER FIVE

TOWARDS OLYMPIC SINGING

Making the most of the voice you have

Having learned something about how to breathe, stand and start the sound, we can now look at ways to *use* your voice — how to develop and build it into a trained instrument capable of whatever the music demands. We shall think about the sound of it, its range and flexibility, its volume, its carrying power and its stamina.

You have the gift of an instrument, and by using the information in the next few chapters, you can learn how to 'play' it.

Before we start, though, I'd like to point out something which could save you a lot of anxiety and wasted time. And that is, that the voice you have now will never change into a 'different' voice. It can certainly be improved, but it will never alter its basic category.

For example, if your present voice is deep and 'dark brown', with a two-octave range from low D, *nothing* you do can change it into the bright voice of a higher tenor or coloratura soprano capable of effortless top C's. I say this because I know dozens of singers (who doesn't?) who imagine themselves in roles for which they are obviously unsuited. Their teachers sometimes encourage them to sing higher or 'bigger' music than they are capable of, with the result that everyone else is embarrassed, the singer disappointed, and the poor voice damaged.

If you can't get within miles of Stevie Wonder's high notes now, you *never* will. And if you get nowhere near the depth of sound or pitch of the lowest voices, you have no chance of ever doing so. Beware of anyone who tells you otherwise! Your voice — its 'colour', its size and its range — has already been manufactured, you cannot swop it for another and nothing you do can radically change it. So be sensible and realistic about your potential, accept your limitations and improve what you *do* have.

Don't be disappointed! There are subtle ways to develop your voice and give you an unfair advantage! Its volume and beauty can be worked on and even its range can expand a note or two.

Let's start with resonance — the resounding or amplification process.

The sound of a piano is not made by the strings alone. When a hammer strikes the strings, the sound created is thrown back and enlarged by a wooden sounding board and this is the sound you hear. Every instrument has an amplifier of some sort. With the acoustic guitar it is the space inside the body of the instrument, and in the human voice it is the space inside you. The vocal cords make the basic sound, which is in fact fairly weak, and this is made louder by the 'tunnel' of the throat, the domed shape of the mouth and the space inside your head.

Everyone says that most singers don't have much between their ears and it's quite true! Look at this drawing:

As you can see, there is a lot of open space *above* the mouth: it is behind the nose, the inside of the nose in fact, and much bigger than you might think.

So the spaces which amplify the basic voice are the throat and mouth and the nose space. The resounding which goes on in these 'echo-chambers' is sometimes called 'chest' resonance and 'nasal' or 'head' resonance. Whatever you decide to call them, these resonances make the sound, and they can be developed to enlarge and beautify it.

The terms 'nasal', 'head' and 'chest' resonance are sometimes misleading: 'nasal' implies an unfortunate voice-characteristic and the chest is *below* the level of the vocal cords. So shall we talk about 'higher' and 'lower' resonance? 'Higher' being the nose space and 'lower' everything else below. This might suggest that the highest notes in your voice are made by the nose resonance only, and the lowest notes come from the throat area. But this would be wrong. All notes in your voice contain resonances from all the spaces — you can't shut off one of them. It is true that one area of resonance tends to be predominant at certain pitches, but it is also true to say that you can control your use of resonance, developing it and 'mixing' it as you wish.

Higher resonance from the nasal space and lower resonance from the throat and mouth space.

Now let's discuss the first.

Higher Resonance

Different sounds have different qualities. The blackbird's song is unlike the sound made by a swan, for instance, and anyone can distinguish a trumpet from a French horn. In a similar way, the resonance of the nasal cavity has a different quality — a different 'colour' — from the resonance of the throat and mouth. It is a brighter sound, 'narrower', more 'pointed' than the lower resonance — like a descant recorder rather than a 'cello. When you have developed it, it will add brightness to your voice — a 'brilliance' which will give it a carrying power. It will also help to keep your singing in tune, and it will give your lower notes a core of focussed sound — a 'point' to the sound which low notes sometimes need to cut through a dense orchestral texture. It is difficult to describe, but you will hear it when it has been developed.

To develop it, you have to become aware of the space behind the nose and start to use it. Humming is the most obvious way to activate it.

Hum on M, N and NG and you will feel that the sound is made in the nasal cavity. Hum up and down scales or on tunes — high and low, loud and soft — feel the bright, higher resonance being used. Put an H before the hum and sing HM — this is possibly better still for activating the nasal air.

Another good exercise is tapping the nose and the cheeks whilst you hum: this seems to stimulate the resonance. Sniffing and blowing out the air in short bursts through your nose both help to identify the space.

All of this develops higher resonance. Perhaps these exercises direct the stream of air from the vocal cords into the nasal space, and in time more of this resonance is naturally added to the sound of your voice. To be honest, I don't know exactly why this happens, but it does. Even in a short time you will notice a difference, and eventually your voice will develop a brighter, resonant quality.

Do as much humming as you wish, throughout your range, on scales, slow and fast — anything you like — it can't damage your voice.

Hum on a note, raise the cheeks into a smiling position, try to get a good buzzing behind the nose, and then open your lips and sing a vowel — EE, or OO if you prefer. The humming seems to 'place' the sound high in the head, and when you open and sing, the high resonance of the hum should continue through into the vowel.

Repeat this, and when you are opening the lips concentrate hard on keeping this high focus in the vowel. Not a nasal sound, but a bright, ringing sound in your voice. It might give you a headache at first: if it does that's fine — you are doing it properly! The headache will disappear.

Do a great deal of this type of practice, but think about it and *concentrate*, making sure that the high focus is there. Feel the bright, ringing quality in the sound — a 'shattering' sensation — like the tinkling sound when you strike a triangle, or the 'ping' when you hit a piece of good cut-glass. Don't force the sound — hum and sing gently at first — let the resonance do the work.

Here's a good exercise:

The aim is to secure a bright, ringing sound throughout. Get a good resonant hum first, gradually open to EE keeping the bright high focus — don't let it drop! Then keep the brightness of the EE into the AH. Breathe whenever you have to.

You'll probably manage to keep the EE focussed high, but AH is more difficult. Some languages, especially English, have flat, dull AH sounds. You may find that the AH 'drops into the mouth'. If it does, it will sound dull and 'hollow' and spoil the line of bright sound. So keep the cheeks high in a smiling position all the time and aim the voice at the bridge of your nose. Eventually you will feel the brilliant, ringing sound which this sort of exercise develops.

Repeat this exercise, concentrating on getting a line of high-placed resonance, a streak of brilliance, a thread of ringing sound permanently in your voice.

This activation of the air inside the nasal space is the only way to guarantee a bright, vibrant sound to your voice. I strongly recommend the practice we have been talking about to all singers, and especially to those with low or dull voices. Experiment with your higher resonance, 'play' with it, in every practice session.

Here is a very useful exercise which will make your voice feel and sound strong and vibrant. It makes *you* feel marvellous, too! It combines breathing, breath control and resonance practice at the same time.

Take a walk for half an hour, at a steady walking pace, breathing in and humming the breath out over a measured number of steps. Support the pressure of the outgoing breath by pulling-in the tummy muscles so that the humming lasts a long time. Hum lightly at a fairly high pitch — long, sustained lines. During the walk, do other resonance-promoting exercises — sniff the air high into your head in short blasts, blow it out the same way, try NG as well as M and N, hum on a middle and a low note. In other words, experiment with the resonance of the nasal cavity.

You will return feeling worn-out, but if you don't collapse, start to sing something you've been working on recently. Your voice will have taken on a new 'bloom' and will be ringing, resonant and vibrant. You will feel that your sound is positioned high and forward — a sensuous and a powerful sensation — a very good feeling! *That* is higher resonance — try it and find out!

Another good exercise for brightening the voice is this, written in the Bass Clef for a bit of sight-reading practice.

Again, the idea is to make a light and bright EE sound — not nasal, but high-placed — a thin strand of sound focussed on the nose. Precede the EE with a hum if it helps. Choose a pitch in the middle of your voice to start. Sing easily, lightly, and feel the resonance in the face. Keep everything relaxed (except your posture) and make sure your larynx is low — don't let it rise.

When you are satisfied with the high-placing of the EE, gradually introduce other vowels, precede them with EE or a hum and transpose the phrase to exercise your full range.

I would like to emphasise again the importance of making the resonance work for you. In your efforts to obtain a high-placed, bright sound, you might be tempted to force the breath pressure. Don't do it — if the resonance isn't right, forcing will not put it right: too much strength will 'over-blow' the sound with harsh or breathy results. Be patient: sing gently, slowly, and concentrate on getting the nasal cavity reverberating with bright sound. It will eventually come easily, and your voice will sound 'bigger' and more resonant than it sounds at the moment — without extra force! *Let the resonance take the strain!*

Going on from this, I would now like to discuss extending this bright, forward sound throughout your vocal range. As I mentioned before, this brightness doesn't have to be *only* in the high notes. There is a tendency for the high resonance to be predominant in high notes, but it is possible, and desirable, to carry it down to the middle and lower notes.

The lower notes in your voice have more lower resonance from the chest area in them, and the higher notes have more of the higher resonance from the head. The low notes sound 'thicker' and the high notes lighter.

What happens, then, when you sing a phrase made up of angular jumps of an octave or more such as this one?

O . . . . .nes (from K. 339)

Adjacent notes will sound alternately 'thick' and light, from the chest and the head, breaking up the smooth line of sound into individual notes of differing quality. An ugly phrase.

And this one by Mozart is mild in comparison with some of his other tunes. We can overcome this problem by singing such phrases with the *same* resonance predominant throughout (some singers would say in the same 'register'). It means, though, that we shall have to develop the ability to carry the high and bright resonance down to our lowest notes. Here's an exercise which will help:

Slow

EE . . . . AH . . . .

The aim is to get a good bright sound on the EE — start with a hum if you wish — and keep the high resonance in your voice down to the lower notes. EE will be easy, but when you change to AH, think high, keep the cheeks raised, get a bright sound. No breathing in the middle, so use the minimum breath. Start this one towards the top of your voice where you can get a bright EE, and gradually transpose the exercise down so that your lower notes have a well-focussed sound.

Exercises like this will develop your ability to sing high and low notes with the same resonance, the same sound, and this means that when you are singing a wide-ranging phrase, you can choose to add the brightness to the lower notes — singing the whole phrase in one 'voice'. You will be able to make a consistent, smooth sound throughout your range, without ugly 'breaks' or 'gear-changes'.

Keeping the brightness in your voice as you sing down a phrase will be easier if you practise singing down a scale in semitones — all the black and white notes on a keyboard — known as a 'chromatic' scale. Perhaps you would compose your own exercise on chromatic scales.

One final point. Well-developed higher resonance will add to the carrying-power of your voice. It gives a core of sound, a 'focus' which carries much better than a 'spread' voice. This means that you will be heard by the people in the back row of the hall and, for those who use a microphone, you can afford to stand further away from it.

Higher resonance is obviously an important part of any singer's technique, so go over this chapter from time to time, practise the exercises, make up some of your own, and work on it until it is right. When it is right, still keep working, because — like a sportsman's technique — if you neglect one aspect of it, even for a month, you will lose that ability.

Lower Resonance

Although the nasal resonance plays an important part in your voice, it is a secondary part. The principal amplifier, which makes the lower resonance, is the throat and mouth space. These are bigger resonators than the nasal cavity and responsible for, perhaps, three-quarters of your sound.

The throat and mouth spaces, then, are the lower resonators and they are helped a little by the chest. I know that the rib-cage is below the level of the vocal cords, but, for some reason, parts of the upper chest seem to vibrate 'in sympathy' with your voice. Some writers have suggested that the bones transmit the sound, and others have thought of the chest cavity as a resonator itself. What the explanation is I don't know, but modern scientific opinion is in favour of some sympathetic vibration from the chest. There is certainly a sensation of chest vibration sometimes: I'm sure you will feel it later on.

The quality of the sound made by the lower resonance is 'broader' than that of the nasal space. As you might expect from more spacious resonators, the sound is 'thicker', heavier, darker, warmer — just as a bassoon's sound is 'fatter' than the 'thinner' quality which the oboe makes.

The sound which your voice makes now is, of course, produced mainly from the throat and mouth: but you may not be using these spaces to their full potential. It is possible to develop the lower resonance to add body and colour to your voice, and the way to do so is by opening these adjustable spaces as wide as comfortable. I have already mentioned dropping the lower jaw to increase your mouth space — all you need to do now is to get into the habit of keeping the throat wide open whilst you are singing.

The tunnel from the Adam's apple (where the cords are) to the back of the throat is adjustable. Feel your throat, or look into a mirror as you swallow and yawn. You can see that the length and width of the column can be altered. For singing, the throat must be as deep and as wide as you can comfortably make it. There are all sorts of ways to reach this deep and wide throat position. One is to yawn, another is to imagine you are about to sneeze, a third sensation is to pretend to swallow a tennis ball, and, if you need one more, try to assume that there is a hot potato in your mouth. All of these will do the same thing: they will expand the width of your throat, raise the roof of your mouth into a more spacious dome, and keep the voice box low.

Try these positions now — easy and relaxed, but with a large cavern of space. Try it with the teeth open just a finger's width, as when you are singing the vowel EE — you can open the throat wide independently of the teeth. Imagine you are yawning and singing at the same time. That's the position for singing.

Open the mouth wide, open the throat wide and deep, and sing a few low notes on AH. The feeling is of being relaxed with a vast amount of available space — like a lofty nave of a cathedral.

Now this position gives the maximum volume of resonating air, so it must become second nature to you if you want body in your voice. (It is impossible to sing all vowels at every pitch with a wide mouth: OO and EE, for example, need a more closed mouth-space. But keep the throat and mouth as comfortably wide as possible whatever you are singing.)

Practise opening the lower resonators while you are singing this phrase:

Slow

Easy and relaxed, with a wide, yawning throat shape, sing on AH first and then try the more closed positions of EE and OO. Sing the exercise in different keys so that all your range is used, and make up a few more easy phrases yourself. Use all the vowels so that you become aware of the space adjustments which have to be made.

The sensation of chest vibration which I mentioned earlier can be felt if you speak or sing on your lowest note. Try to imitate a cat's purring or the z-z-z-z-z-buzzing made by a bumble-bee.

You will feel this sympathetic vibration in the upper chest and the lower part of your neck, as though your chest itself is vibrating — rather like the floor shaking when heavy rock music or a large church organ is being played.

If you do this buzzing on a low note, feel the chest vibration and open your mouth and sing AH, your sound will have a new dark, heavy and powerful quality which gives the impression of being lower in pitch than it actually is. (If you have ever heard those 'black' Russian bass voices, it's *that* sort of deep sound. It seems to have a 'cutting edge' — and it carries.)

All voices can feel some of this chest quality, and by developing it, another useful 'colour' can be added to your repertoire of sounds. It broadens and darkens your voice — useful in some dramatic and sombre phrases — and it can be carried up to the higher notes if you want a bigger sound up there. Practise it by working on the bumble-bee buzzing in the chest, or the purring if that is easier, until you can feel the vibration and then open on to a vowel — AH is a good one for this. Develop this sensation and add it to all the vowels in the bottom few notes of your voice. When you have developed the ability to add this chest quality to your lowest note at will, try to carry it up into the middle notes of your range with this exercise:

Pitch the exercise so that the lowest note is the bottom note of your voice. The key in which I've written it, B flat, is suitable for fairly high voices, say mezzo-sopranos or tenors. Lower voices will need to sing it in F or E flat.

Start with a secure bumble-bee buzzing or cat's purring sensation in the upper chest. When you feel the chest vibration strongly, open your mouth wide — don't lose the vibration — and sing AH. Then carry the chest resonance into every note of the exercise.

When you are satisfied with these five notes, extend the phrase to an octave or more to add weight to your middle and upper notes. (Not too high — your top three or four notes shouldn't be attempted from the chest — you might strain your voice.)

There is some manuscript paper at the end of this chapter for your own exercises. Use all the vowels, not only AH, and carry the lower resonance of the chest up towards your higher notes.

We seem to have spent a lot of time talking about resonance, but I hope you have found it interesting. It is certainly an important part of your vocal technique — perhaps the most important — because it makes your sound, its carrying power and its variety of expressive 'colourings'. All of this stuff about nasal spaces, yawning and bumble-bees in your chest — these things make your voice!

Work on this chapter, as much as you can for as long as you like. I promise you will be pleased with the improvement, and I guarantee you'll get plenty of compliments!

Range

Before going on to some vocal gymnastics, I want to discuss briefly the compass of the voice.

As I mentioned earlier, the voice you have now is unlikely to change dramatically, either in type or in range. The vocal apparatus which was given to you at birth is fully developed by the late 'teens — there are very, very few cases of a voice changing its compass or its category after that age. I know of one case — and that is a very special voice, anyway.

You can accept that the range you have now is roughly the range you will always have. Sorry to disappoint you if you have hopes of singing high C's and all you can manage, with a struggle, is an E flat. But that is the situation. To try to 'correct' Nature's intentions to that extent will wreck your voice.

Your natural range should be about two octaves or a little less. That's about thirteen or fourteen consecutive white notes on a piano. All these notes may not be comfortable yet, but you can develop your technique so that you can sing them easily. And two octaves is enough for almost everything you will be asked to sing. All popular songs can easily be sung with this range, and the arias and recitatives of opera and oratorio are always written for specific voice-types, all of which have, and always have had, this compass.

These voice types in so-called 'classical' music are known as soprano, contralto, tenor and bass. There are some variations — mezzo-soprano and baritone amongst others — but the natural range-categories are these four: S, A, T and B.

The soprano's range is about two octaves upwards from middle C, the contralto's about four white notes lower, i.e. F to F. In male voices, the tenor is roughly an octave lower than the soprano, and the range of the bass an octave lower than the contralto. All give or take a note or two.

This is in 'classical' music: in none of the other types of singing are these categories used, but all voices, male and female, whatever sort of music you sing, should fall into these ranges.

Your natural range, then, if your voice is healthy, should be about thirteen or fourteen white notes. A few lucky people have a note or two extra, but I've never heard of a person in good health who is not capable of making some sound on twelve or thirteen consecutive notes.

I say 'some sound' because the invariable difficulty about range is not that you can't sing a wide enough range, but that you can't sing it comfortably. And that is a problem of technique, not of range. 'Short-range' voices appear not to be too common: badly-produced voices, on the other hand, can be heard sometimes!

If your techniques of attack, breathing and resonance are easy and relaxed, you shouldn't have any complaints about most of your range. The extremes of your voice, top and bottom, may not be right yet, but they will be in time.

It seems, then, that real problems about our upper and lower notes very rarely exist: the only problems we have are: (1) that some notes are uncomfortable, especially high and low notes, and (2) that songs are printed in a 'middling' key unsuitable for some voices. The first is temporary — we can develop our technique to sing all notes in our range easily — and the second problem can be removed immediately, by transposing the music into a more comfortable key.

If you feel that your range needs to be worked on, start now on a programme designed to perfect your vocal technique. Concentrate on easy, relaxed attack, breath control and resonance — these three in particular — and work first in the comfortable section of your voice. Start with the exercises mentioned in previous chapters, and sing them in the lower and middle parts of your voice — about an eight-note compass. Gradually, over a few weeks or months, extend the range of these technique-perfecting exercises to include the upper notes. If your singing is correct when you sing middle and lower pitches, you won't have difficulty with the higher notes in time.

You can't shift the natural span of your voice, then. If you have a tenor range, trying to lower your pitch to sing the bottom bass notes will be unsuccessful and it will take away the ability to control the upper notes, and vice versa. You can't 'stretch' your voice to that extent, but it is possible to improve your control of singing the highest and lowest notes.

As far as the highest notes are concerned, you will find that sustained high-pitched humming over a period will make the top of your voice feel less of a struggle. The humming puts your voice on a higher level — it makes the top few notes more secure. Try humming or singing a vowel on one of your top notes, quietly — if you can't sing it quietly, you shouldn't be singing it at all. Keep the breath pressure low but well supported, and sustain the sound for twenty or more seconds.

That sort of exercise will help a lot, and here's another good one:

Fairly quick

AH . . . .

This phrase spans twelve notes, so start on your lowest comfortable note, and you should be able to sing it easily. If you can, transpose the exercise up a semitone at a time until your highest notes are reached. Progress gradually, and don't raise the pitch unless the previous key is comfortable.

If you can't cope easily with a twelfth, start on something less demanding, such as this:

AH _____

Again move on *only* when all the notes are comfortable.

As with all exercises in this work-book, these two are for your voice, not mine, so sing them in keys suitable for you, transposing them if necessary. Compose similar phrases yourself and sing them on every vowel.

To sing your lowest notes easily is less of a problem. Generally speaking, there is much less difficulty with lower notes — it is the top few semitones which provide the split notes and the red faces! We can, though, do some useful work on the bottom of our voices to give those low notes an impressive security and strength.

As with the upper notes, humming on low pitches over a period of time will stabilize those bottom few semitones which at present might be shaky. Try it over a period of about a week as an experiment — especially if you are having some trouble with low notes. Grumble away on hums and vowels, at the bottom end of your voice: sing over a range of about a fifth. You'll be surprised at the ease of your low notes in the following week!

The real secret of getting your low range right is relaxation and space. Lots of people start to push from the throat down there, only to constrict the throat space. Yawn and relax, give the notes a lot of space, bring in the resonance of the chest — this is the way to get the most from your bottom notes. Try this on a simple phrase — here's one:

Slow

AH   AH   AH   AH   AH

The bottom note should be your lowest. Easy, relaxed and spacious all the way down — no forcing. Start with the wide vowels, and then try the more closed EE and OO.

The exercises we have talked about in this section will help your range at least a little. Although there is no way to stretch your voice more than a note or two, this type of practice will add a noticeable security to your upper and lower extremes. You will develop increased control over phrases which lie high in your voice, and the low notes will 'tell' clearly. Two octaves of well produced and comfortable sounds is what to aim for: with this range you can manage any music which is worth singing.

Agility — Athletics — Gymnastics

So far we have talked only about slow-moving and sustained phrases, both of which are most important in establishing a sound vocal technique. All styles of singing require more from your ability than this, however: whatever type of music you sing, there will be occasions when you have to sing fast-moving passages, trills, 'decorations', runs, scales and so on — music which demands vocal flexibility.

In popular music, there are lots of little 'ornaments' on some of the notes, such as 'blue' notes, 'bent' notes and grace notes. However the sort of passage which really tests your fitness is this type:

Fast

re - joice _____ great - ly

Every choir-singer will immediately recognise this as one of the many tricky passages from Handel's 'Messiah'. Vocal flexibility of this sort is a prerequisite of singing, especially in the case of seventeenth and eighteenth – century music.

The principal point to remember is that to sing any phrase which requires speed or agility, you have to use a light 'touch'. The heavy, lower resonance voice you would use to sing broad, sustained passages just won't move that quickly, any more than the super-heavy-weight-lifters could compete in the 100-metres hurdles. So you have to lighten the voice, think high, use the upper resonance in all agility singing. When practising any difficult phrases like the last example, slow down the tempo a little to a speed you can manage, and gradually increase the speed. A metronome would be a useful investment for this.

The most common type of phrase you need to work on is the fast-moving, scale-like run, and almost without exception it is a decoration of a simple tune. The one from 'The Messiah', for example, is a more elaborate version of this:

If you look closely at all runs, you will notice a tune somewhere in the middle of all those dots. Bear that in mind when you sing any long florid passages, and try to emphasise the tune. This will give the line a purpose, a direction without which the passage would be dull.

Here are two exercises to show you how to practise:

The aim is to articulate all the notes clearly, but sing a phrase, not individual notes, giving it some movement or direction with accents on each group of four or eight notes, to emphasise the 'melody'. In the second exercise, for example, the 'tune' notes are the first of each group of four — a major scale — so accent each first note to give the line impetus, and don't forget to use the light head-voice.

Take passages like this from your repertoire, and break them down into simple tunes. Sing the tunes first, then add the decoration notes slowly, gradually building up the tempo to the correct speed. You will find this sort of practice a great help in developing your ability to sing fast-moving notes neatly.

The other note groups which come under this section are the trill, the turn, the mordent, and a few more — some of them a bit complicated — which you can find under the heading 'Ornaments' in any good music dictionary. They are all variations of little 'shakes' on adjacent notes much favoured by eighteenth-century composers, and used in a simpler form today — sometimes extremely attractively — by the best popular singers. This is what they look like:

THE TRILL   THE TURN   THE MORDENT

They all have a similar function, that of embellishing or decorating a note by a rapid repetition of the note and its adjacent notes.

In practising these ornaments, you should again avoid the heavy chest-voice and the aim must be to articulate the notes clearly without slowing down their fast pace. Remember that they are decorative groups, not essential melody notes.

Performing these ornaments properly has to be developed by working up the speed gradually from a slow starting pace. Start on an exercise such as this:

Slow

for the trill and something similar, which you might like to compose yourself, for the turn.

A metronome would be a help here: start slowly at about crotchet=60, and gradually increase the speed to crotchet=120. These note groups are only a few of the decorations in use. There are others in groups of three, five and six, and you could also include staccato notes and wider intervals in your practice.

If you would like to do some research, how about looking up the other ornaments? Compose some exercises based on them, and chart your progress in singing them neatly at increasing speeds. There are enough blank pages at the end of this chapter for your graphs, charts and exercises.

SUMMARY/NOTES/CHARTS

CHAPTER SIX

ARTICULATION — COMMUNICATION

Making Yourself Understood in any Language

This neglected aspect of vocal training can become extremely complicated. It is a wide and an involved subject to which a whole book could be devoted, but I shall try to select only the most important areas, and simplify the information necessary for singing.

The important topics are vowels, diphthongs, consonants and legato singing.

Vowels

So far, I have been spelling the vowels in English — AH, EE, OO. Now I would like you to forget these spellings and get used to their Latin equivalents, which are internationally accepted amongst singers.

The five Italian vowels are: I E A O U — and this is how they sound in English:

I   as in ch*ee*se
E   as in *e*ver
A   as in g*a*rden
O   as in f*o*r
U   as in f*oo*l

These five sounds are the basis of the vowels of all western languages. I would like to add three more:

Ü   no equivalent in English, but in German bl*ü*then and in French p*u*pitre
ER as in h*er*
Á   as in h*a*t

These eight vowel sounds make up almost one hundred per cent of the sounds in any language in which we have to sing.

It is very easy to fall into the habit of singing indistinctly without being aware of it. If this happens, the listener will not only be unable to understand the words, he will also find the singing lacking in clarity and variety. We have to exaggerate the different vowel colours so that they are all distinct and pure.

Shall we go through them individually, and point out their different characteristics?

I   — as in ch*ee*se is often impure. It can sound more like Ü sometimes, and it can become nasal. It should be bright and wide. When you practise on this vowel, experiment with the position of the lips: make sure they are open wide enough, and aim for a wide, bright and resonant sound. A cassette recorder would help you to identify any imperfections, which we don't often notice when we are singing.

E   — as in *e*ver must be clearly different from ER. It is a wider and a clearer sound than ER. It needs wide mouth space, more air: think of 'air' when you sing it. When practising it, precede it with I (I-E) to give it more brightness, try to raise the upper jaw to give it space and you will make a good pure vowel sound. Whenever you are trying to brighten your sounds, don't drop the bottom jaw wide, but imagine the upper jaw is opening upwards. (The upper jaw doesn't move, of course, it is fixed, but the sensation helps.)

A   — as in g*a*rden can be a problem for non-Latin singers, because it is often spoken as a dull, flat sound. Compare the English 'f*a*ther' with its Italian equivalent 'Giov*a*nni', and you will see what I mean. When it is dull, it will ruin a line of bright, resonant sound, so some of us have to work on it. The tongue has to be flat in the bottom of the mouth for this vowel too.

In practice, then, work on a bright Italian A, plenty of mouth space and a flat tongue.

If you can make a resonant I sound, precede the A with it and keep them both bright. In fact, I - E - A makes a useful exercise.

O — as in for is generally a well-behaved vowel — few people have difficulty with it. Make sure your tongue is flat and towards the top notes give O plenty of mouth space as you would with A.

U — as in fool can be very difficult! Many singers have difficulty with it. If your lips are pouted forward, it becomes 'breathy' and fails to carry, and it can sometimes be nasal. To get a good resonant U needs a lot of work for most people. In practice, don't push the lips too far forward, and experiment with high resonance without making a nasal sound.
Preceding it with M, N and NG and with the vowel I will help.

Ü — as in the German blü then or the French pu pitre is a useful and easy sound, if you can pronounce it! It is halfway between I and U if that helps or, better still, ask a Frenchman or a German to teach you how to say it. This isn't a harsh or bright sound — it's a soft, warm vowel, a lovely sound, and easy to sing. You will have to pout your lips to sing it properly.
Precede it with some chest resonance exercises, and you will make a beautiful warm sound.

ER — as in her is rarely sung well — making 'girl' sound like 'garl' and 'world' like 'warld'. If you open your mouth too much, it will be impossible to pronounce ER purely. It needs only a moderate space, with the lips a little forward. As I mentioned earlier, when singing this vowel, the tongue, mouth, jaw and throat are in a very relaxed state, and for this reason you should be able to make a clear, pure sound on it.

Á — as in hat is another which can easily be mispronounced, making 'and', for example, sound 'ahnd'. It should be an easy sound — it needs a lot of space and a wide, bright sound. Precede it with I to help its brightness.

Those are all the vowels, then, and here is a bit more advice about perfecting them. All vowels are made by the vocal cords: the lips and mouth have little to do with their formation. They only refine the sounds. The different vowel sounds are created by the voice-box — before they get as far as the mouth. If you want proof of this, open the teeth just a finger's width and pronounce all the vowels. They are made at the moment of attack. So, in practice, concentrate on a clear vowel made by the vocal cords, and don't think too much about the lips.

Diphthongs

Most languages, although not Italian, have diphthongs or vowel mixtures. The English word 'join' is made up of two vowels, O and I — and the word 'game' has the mixture of E and I. There are hundreds of examples in English which we sing every day without noticing these two-vowel sounds. Here are some more: hate (E-I), go (O-U), shine (A-I), house (A-U), poor (U-ER).

Each of the eight vowels needs a *slightly* different throat and mouth adjustment. Touch your Adam's apple whilst you sing the vowels, and you will feel the movements of the larynx as well as the adjustments of the jaw and lips. Each has a different position, hasn't it? And unless these movements are made deliberately, they are not made distinctly enough to produce clear and pure vowels. (This is also true of speaking.)

When you sing a diphthong, then, a vocal adjustment has to be made on the second vowel, and the purity of the two vowels will represent your vocal mobility. It takes conscious adjustment to produce a good diphthong, and so I recommend that you practise singing these pairs of vowel mixtures.

As there are eight vowels, there must be quite a lot of different diphthong possibilities. Perhaps you could work out all the combinations and compose exercises on vowel mixing. Here is one to start you off:

I-E   I-A   I-O   I-U   I-Ü   I-ER   I-Á   I-E

The other point about diphthongs is that their two vowels should be in speech-rhythm to make them sound natural. When we speak a diphthong we put emphasis on the first vowel and not on the second: the first sound is also the longer. In 'shine', for example, the accent and the length is on A and I is less important. But when shine is sung, we often hear:

SHA — I   —   NE.

with the second vowel taking up most of the length. I think this is ugly. In speech, it would sound something like this:

| SHA | INE |

Most of the emphasis and length is on the first vowel, the second is placed at the end to articulate the word clearly. So, when this word is sung more intelligently, it sounds something like this:

SHA — INE.

Think about diphthongs, and experiment to find their best articulation.

Consonants

The trouble with consonants is that if you don't bother with them enough, your words won't be understood, and if you attach too much importance to them, your line of sound will be badly broken. They should be clear but unobtrusive — pronounced distinctly and quickly — and this requires some flexibility of the tongue, throat and lips.

If the clothes-line is the smooth phrase you are singing, the consonants should be the clothes-pegs. The vowels make the sound, and the consonants should make the words intelligible without interfering too much with the line of sound.

Like this   `C| V |C`   not this   `C | V | C`

All languages have enough consonants to cause trouble, but German really is a menace! Look at this passage from a Schubert song:

Hoff - nungs leer   ver schallt die Kla — ge

It's difficult enough to speak, but when you are singing you really have to work hard to pronounce these clusters of consonants clearly and quickly without spoiling the smoothness of the phrase. And, of course, they have to be fitted in *before* the beat. In the word 'Klage', the A is sounded *on* the first beat, and so K and L have to be placed just before it.

This sort of thing needs lots of slow practice — and patience!

Another aspect of consonants, and one which is sometimes overlooked, is that some of them have a pitch — they have to be 'sung' on a particular note. Sing L, for instance, and you will detect a note. Not many consonants have a pitch, most of them are enunciated by the throat, tongue, lips and teeth, as with K, T and F. But five of them do have a pitch: they are L, M, N, R and Z. (V and W might also be included.) These consonants are sometimes called 'voiced' or 'pitched' consonants.

The problem to be avoided when singing these five consonants is that of singing them at a different pitch from the vowel which follows —

Lord

If you sing the L of Lord at a different pitch from the OR, as often happens, an ugly 'scoop' is heard. It sounds like this:

L — ord

All of the voiced consonants can cause this trouble, but the worst is the rolled R. R has to be rolled a little, and it makes a fairly loud noise. So when it is voiced on a different note from the following vowel, it's a terrible sound! Be particularly aware of this sort of thing:

Rex   tre-men - dae ma   - je - sta - tis

These two rolled R's, in the well-known phrase from the Verdi 'Requiem' are very exposed. An ugly glissando on the first two notes would certainly be an embarrassment at the play-back!

If you haven't been aware of voiced consonants before, or if you would like to improve your singing of them, practise these five consonants on pitches — following them with a suitable vowel. Like this:

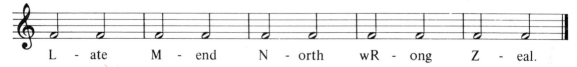

L - ate   M - end   N - orth   wR - ong   Z - eal.

When the consonant and the vowel can be sung at the same pitch, reduce the length of the consonant to its natural duration.

Two points about consonants, then: clear, crisp articulation, and some of them in pitch. Only small details, but they add enormously to your singing.

To cover all the over 8,000 different languages and dialects in current use in the world, an encyclopaedia of books and a cleverer person than I would be required. But the vowels and consonants we have talked about will cover most of the languages in which you will be asked to sing. Until we are all speaking Esperanto, then, if you speak, or have to sing a language which contains vowels and consonants not mentioned here, add the extra vowels and consonants to your exercises and work on them in your practice sessions.

Legato Singing

Finally in this section, we can include legato singing — another facet of musicianship and vocal skill which is sometimes lacking — even amongst the best singers.

Legato means smooth and unbroken: it's the opposite of staccato, which is short and detached. These two opposite styles of performing music are demonstrated by a sustaining instrument, such as the organ, and a percussive one, such as tubular bells or a xylophone. The first makes a long, smooth, sustained sound, and the percussive instrument is struck, making disconnected notes which fade away immediately.

Because vocal music is concerned with the meaning of words, and not only with sounds, we have to sing *phrases* of words, not individual words — phrases of sound, not individual notes. Legato singing is intelligent singing, and we must always sing sustained phrases except when the composer wants staccato for an effect.

I know there are lots of other things to think about when you are singing, like tempo, pitch, vowels and watching the conductor, but if you can sing a steady, sustained, expansive line of sound, it's marvellous to listen to — and to sing!

Here's a phrase which seems to cause difficulty. I've never heard it sung smoothly yet:

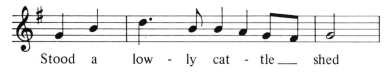

Stood   a   low - ly   cat - tle ___ shed

The first three notes of this phrase from the carol 'Once in Royal David's City' *must* be sustained, otherwise the words are disjointed like this — stood, a, low, ly — as though the notes were being struck on a xylophone. It's always badly sung: listen for it next Christmas! And if you ever have to sing it, sing it like an organ, not like church bells.

Whilst we are on the subject of Christmas music, I'd like to point out another difficult phrase — partly because it's a useful example, but also because it's an extremely beautiful carol. It is a French traditional Christmas song called 'Quelle est cette odeur agréable', and it starts like this:

Quelle est cette   o - deur   a - gre   a - ble,   Ber - gers. Qui

ra - vit   tous nos   sens?

45

This is difficult because the phrases are long and because there are lots of jumps in the tune — always hard to sing smoothly. If we could chart the volume of our line when we sing a phrase like this, and indeed we can by looking at the 'recording level' of a home tape recorder, there would be a lot of high points, rather like those electro-cardiogram screens which monitor heartbeats. We have to smooth out those peaks by sustaining the level of sound — singing *through* the phrase right until the last note, sustaining the breath pressure.

When you are singing phrases like this, don't sing isolated notes. Sustain the sound with constant breath support, sing through the phrase, keep the last note in mind — that's where the phrase is going to. And if you are running out of breath two-thirds of the way through — crescendo, support the sound, keep it strong to the last note.

To show yourself how super-smooth a phrase can be, even when it is angular like the last example, hum the tune. Not individual notes, but one long, sustained line of sound, unbroken, with no 'daylight' between the notes. Try it! The sound doesn't stop — it is continuous. Try to get that 'length' of sound in all phrases.

Something else you could try is singing phrases without the consonants — which, of course, interrupt the flow of sound. Sing only the vowels. Try this with 'Amazing Grace' the words are: 'Amazing Grace, how sweet the sound, that saved a wretch like me', but sing only the vowel sounds, like this:

It might sound a bit stupid, but it's very useful to emphasise the 'strength' of a smooth line.

Easier than this, and possibly smoother still, is singing phrases from your repertoire on one vowel — removing all the hindrances and just concentrating on making a marvellously smooth line. Choose some phrases from the music you sing, or use this — the first four bars from Johnny Mandel's 'The shadow of your smile':

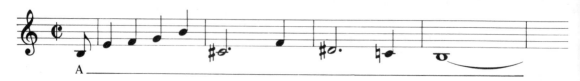

Notice how smooth a line can be and, when you later add the words, try to sing it just as legato as you did without the words.

The long ascending and descending scale is a good line on which to develop legato singing, and it builds vocal stamina too.

Slow

I often draw arrows or phrase marks in red pencil across long phrases as a visual reminder to sing T H R O U G H the line to the last note. When you are practising this exercise, keep sustaining the sound, expand it, don't let it die away, especially towards the end. Sing it in all keys on every vowel.

All this is fine, but we don't only sing sounds, we have to sing words. And words include not only consonants to interrupt the smooth flow of sound, but also natural verbal accentuation which is another problem.

Verbal accents are the natural stresses, or emphasis, some syllables have in normal speaking. In this sentence, the natural accents are underlined and in speaking or singing, these stresses help to make the words and the meaning understood. The dramatic Italian language seems to have an accent in every word, usually on the penultimate syllable. This emphasis, which is often accompanied by gestures, is an essential part of the language, and without it the language wouldn't make sense, even to Italians.

All languages have rise and fall, strong and weak, volume and rhythmic variety, and this colourfulness must be brought out in singing. The natural word accents must be preserved in the legato line — some syllables have to be emphasised, without making the smooth phrase too 'lumpy'. And this requires some thought. You have to build a little, lean towards the verbal accents, within the framework of the sustained line. Give occasional emphasis within the consistently sustained phrase, known as 'marcato' within legato.

I'll show you an example:

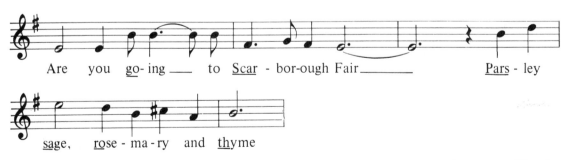

This well-known folk song has legato lines, and although there is a lilt, the phrases have to be sustained — not with a regular 'beat' as in a waltz. The word accents have to be decided by the singer, but I think they are those which I have underlined.

47

Now, you have to *lean slightly* on these accents — but not so strongly that the other notes aren't heard. All the notes are important, they must all be sustained, but the natural word emphasis should be felt. All the syllables, whether strong or weak, should be sustained in a smooth line, but the phrase has to work towards the verbal accents, making them *slightly* prominent. It is difficult, so it needs a lot of thought and practice with a tape-recorder, and an acute ear.

This verbal accentuation within a legato line is especially important in recitative — a style of singing based on speech rhythm. Look it up if you aren't familiar with it, and, if you are unsure about where the correct verbal accents fall, look that up too, in a dictionary.

As well as word accents, we have to think about musical accents. Not all notes have the same volume — some music is accented in groups of three notes, like the waltz, some in four like the march, and so on. Hence the different styles according to their rhythm or 'feel' — bossa nova, saraband, polka, jig, minuet and fandango all have different patterns of musical accents. Some notes are stressed — some are not. Vocal music is no exception.

All songs have a musical rhythm as well as word rhythm, and, in the best vocal writing, the two coincide — (song-writers, take note).

If you go   then I'll   be   blue   'cos brea-kin' up is hard   to   do__

In these three bars from 'Breaking-up is Hard To Do', the natural word-stresses, which are underlined, have been placed by the composer on the natural musical accents. This makes a satisfying unity between words and music. Had the verbal accents been placed on the second and fourth beats of the bar, the music would have been uncoordinated and unsingable.

Well-written vocal music like this is relatively easy to sing, but not all composers are as helpful to singers as Neil Sedaka is. When you come across word and musical accents which don't synchronise, you have to decide which is more important and compromise. I would favour the words and let their natural accents determine the rhythm of the music.

Composers who have a genius for words and singing write the best vocal music. If you would like to sing some of the greatest music for the voice, get hold of music by John Dowland, Monteverdi, Henry Purcell, Schubert, Verdi and Benjamin Britten, most of whom were singers.

One of my favourite composers, Peter Warlock, was so concerned about the importance of words that he wrote at the top of one of his songs — 'To be sung as though unbarred, i.e. phrased according to the natural accentuation of the words, especially avoiding an accent on the first beat of the bar when no accent is demanded by the sense.' The song is called 'Sleep', and its piano accompaniment played alone has almost no natural rhythm — the words entirely determining the accents of the music.

I would strongly recommend a thorough study of Warlock's songs to any singer or song-writer who is interested in sensitive and perceptive vocal music. And amongst modern popular song-writers I would suggest The Carpenters, Neil Sedaka and Elton John for similar reasons.

The practice of writing music divided into neat and regular bars which are supposed to indicate its rhythm, is a relatively recent phenomenon in the history of written music. It has been done for about 400 years. We don't need these bar lines and time signatures to tell us where the accents are — we can 'feel' them. The bar lines' usefulness is in helping the appearance of printed music — in making it easier to read. Tunes written to words often don't fall easily into these rigid compartments — they are irregularly accented and need rhythmic freedom to express themselves fluently.

For this reason, the 'fundamental' vocal music on which to base and with which to compare all other sung music, is the plainsong of the early church. This is singing at its most free, most natural and its most expressive. There were no accompaniments, no bar lines, no time signatures, no conductors and no producers! A singer's paradise! The melodies and rhythms were uncomplicated, and the familiar Latin words of the liturgy were simply intoned mostly on adjacent notes within a small range at a comfortable pitch.

That is *real* singing — basic singing — because its simplicity allows the singer freedom to express what should be expressed, namely, the beauty of line, sound and the natural interpretation of the words. To sing it is very good news — it is lovely music, and a new 'dimension' in singing — even though much of it is a thousand years old!

Do look into it and learn how to sing it, and if you know of a monastery which still practises the daily office, make a bee-line for it.

Finally, in this chapter, I would like to mention some points which might help you to sing awkward tunes more smoothly. Adjacent notes are fairly easy, but tunes which contain wide intervals — or jumps — can be very difficult.

Singing intervals legato can best be practised by starting with fairly small jumps of about three notes, slurring or sliding your voice between the two. Like this:

SLIDE   SLIDE   SLIDE   SLIDE   SLIDE   SLIDE

Work slowly at first, making a deliberate glissando, or slide, between the two notes. Be careful of the pitch of the notes, they can easily become flat. Quicken the speed of the slide until it is so fast that it isn't noticed. That will be the shortest distance between two notes, making a smooth movement.

When you can sing thirds legato, move on to bigger intervals and make up similar exercises, using all vowels throughout your range.

Three examples of tunes which contain some awkward intervals, and are therefore difficult to sing smoothly, are 'The way we were', 'Bless the beasts and the children', and the hymn 'The Day Thou Gavest':

This type of phrase sometimes sounds as though it is being played by one finger on the piano — with isolated and disconnected notes. It should be one long, smooth phrase. Elongate the vowels of the fourth bar so there is no 'daylight' between them, and they will become one 'unit of sound', not unrelated notes.

Again those intervals must be sung smoothly in long phrases. Any singer would find it difficult, and, unless his technique of singing intervals and arpeggios smoothly has been perfected by practice, he will make a mess of it. (Arpeggios, by the way, are the chords which are 'spread' or played one note at a time as a harp would play them. The third, fourth and fifth notes of this example form an arpeggio.) When you have to sing angular phrases like this smoothly, work hard in your training periods on humming the tune, singing it on one vowel: draw arrows across the words, aim for the last note — and anything else you can think of to fuse together the individual notes into one unit of sound.

The hymn tune I mentioned is this one:

— another up and down line which needs a long, sustained approach. Imagine it played by the violin section of an orchestra — a big, sweeping melody — that's how you should sing it.

If you don't sing it smoothly, your audience will hear twelve isolated and unrelated notes, one at a time, some high, some low — chosen at random almost! As in this graph:

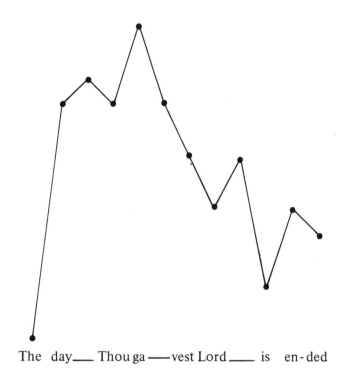

The day___ Thou ga ——vest Lord ___ is en-ded

This shows the distance of the jumps and the tempo of the tune — 'ping-pong' music — and tunes made up of wide intervals can easily sound as disjointed as the graph looks. But if the graph is 'stretched' horizontally, and you think of the phrase as one line, they both become less angular and more shapely:

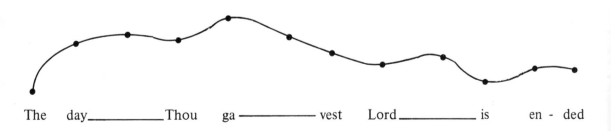

The   day_____Thou   ga ——————— vest   Lord_____ is   en - ded

You have to 'elongate' the phrase: don't worry about high notes, sing *through* the line to the last note.

Articulation for singers is a more complicated subject than it first appears to be. And it isn't noticed only when it is done badly — the audience sits up and listens when you articulate well. Good, intelligent singing has to be developed, thought about and practised — you have to put a lot into it. But when you do, the people in the audience don't only hear, they *listen* — and that is light years away from being just another vocalist.

I hope you work on this chapter, think about it, have some ideas of your own and put them into practice.

Here is a page for your notes, and one for composing your own exercises.

NOTES/SUMMARY

CHAPTER SEVEN

TRAINING SESSIONS — HOW TO PRACTISE

I'd like to make a few points about how to get the best results from the time you have available — and I hope you can manage some free time regularly because this section assumes you are prepared to put as much into singing as you get out of it — whether it earns your living or not.

For some strange reason, a lot of singers never get down to regular practising. Perhaps singing is thought of as a 'natural' thing to do, like walking, swimming and running, something which can be done easily — anytime. And for some people, it is. But, if you want to do it well, if you want to develop your talent and do justice to the music, you'll have to dedicate yourself to it as much as the competitive swimmers and runners do. Accomplished intrumentalists practise every day, so do athletes — and so do the best singers.

The object of daily practising is to develop fully your potential and to perfect every detail of vocal technique so that at your rehearsals, concerts and recordings, the mechanics of your voice are *always* reliable. Having that degree of skill gives you confidence and you can then enjoy the music and relax into its meaning. Your importance to the listener shouldn't be reduced by your musical and vocal problems.

Your ambition should be a perfect and easy technique which is second-nature to you and which you don't have to worry about. Here are some rules — all of them important.

1. *Warming up*. Like the athlete's body, the voice has to be gently warmed up to work at its best and to avoid damage. Singing energetically from 'cold', especially at the top of the voice, is guaranteed to produce a rough sound. Ten minutes of slow, quiet and gentle warming up should be enough. Do some humming, use the bottom octave first, practise easy attack, opening the throat, breath control exercises and sustained notes.

2. *Posture*. Avoid the temptation of sitting at a keyboard or other instrument to accompany yourself — at least for some of the practice period.

3. *Use real music* as well as exercises. Take phrases from your repertoire and use them to improve any technical details.

4. *Not too long*, especially for beginners and young singers. The muscles of the throat and larynx can become tired and start to ache. Twenty minutes, two or three times a day, is normally enough at first.

5. *'Think seven times and sing once'* an old teacher of mine said. What he meant was that you should have a purpose in singing every phrase rather then haphazardly singing through exercises over and over again. Remember the object of the exercise — to perfect your technique — to perfect every phrase in every way. The vowel, the breath, the support, the pitch, the posture, the attack, the sound — concentrate on these things and your singing will improve quickly.

6. *The lowest octave first.* Don't over-use the highest part of your voice until the middle and lower notes are easy and well produced. And even then move only gradually towards the top.

7. *Quiet singing* has to be right before you can sing loudly. *Slow singing* has to be right before you can sing fast.

8. *Gestures.* Some people make gestures when they speak. The hands, arms and head are moved to emphasise a point or as a natural reaction to the meaning of the words. If you find it natural to do so, fine! After all, it is words and their meaning which we are singing as well as crotchets and quavers. So express yourself with your body in public and in practice sessions to the extent which you feel is natural and acceptable. I think this is preferable to standing rigid like a statue.

9. *Regular practice.* One hour a day has always been more effective than seven hours on Sunday. It doesn't matter what stage you are at now — *regular* practice is the only way to maintain and develop your ability. Singing is a physical activity — it uses muscles and breath — and like any other physical training, if you have practised it daily for a few weeks, it will be noticeably fitter. Your voice can develop flexibility, agility, strength and stamina.

10. *Practise with a friend* once in a while. Your ears can become accustomed to little faults and you will overlook them. Get someone else to listen to you occasionally — the other person's ear will be more perceptive of your singing than your own.

11. *Don't sing on a full stomach.* (Is anyone still eating big meals?) If you feel uncomfortably full of food, the muscles used in breathing and breath control will be prevented from moving freely. You always sing better emptier than fuller.

12. *Commit yourself* to healthy and beautiful singing.

You probably won't have a lot of time to waste, so instead of going through songs and exercises at random in your training periods, why not do the job effectively by planning your work? I will help you to make a practice schedule which will be very helpful if you stick to it.

We'll start with a comprehensive chart in case you have the time and the desire to cover the practice thoroughly. This chart includes all the details of the technical requirements of singing, so, if you follow it closely, your voice should be in tremendous shape — always.

	DAY 1	2	3	4	5	6	7	8	9	10	11	12	13	14	15	16
Resonance	✓					25										
Breath	✓	OR IN				15										
Attack and ending the note	✓	MINUTES				15										
Articulation	✓					35										
Range	✓					10										
Agility	✓					20										

These six headings cover the total extent of your technique. They all have sub-headings, of course. Breath, for instance, includes super breathing and breath control, and Articulation has the sub-headings of vowel purity, legato and consonants, to mention just a few.

In every practice session, you have to work on exercises from each of the sub-headings, so that every detail of your technique gets at least a few minutes' work-out every day. It takes a big slice out of the day, I know, and it becomes complex — but if you can manage it, you'll be surprised by the improvement.

Spend an equal amount of time on each heading — say twenty minutes (two hours during the day). In this twenty minutes, practise all the important items under that heading, using my exercises and your own, and tick the square or record the minutes, when you have completed the work.

If you think one of the headings is unnecessary for you, divide your time between five headings, and if you think some areas of your singing need more work than others, allocate your time proportionately.

Devise your own chart based on the one above.

This extent of effort is only for the most dedicated singers with the time to spare. For those with less time we can make a simpler chart. Some of the technical points can be combined in one exercise to save time. These are some of the combinations:

Attack with vowel purity.
Humming with breath control.
Agility with range.

Here is a suggestion for a more simple combination chart — useful for singers with a limited amount of practice time:

The combinations	DAY 1	2	3	4	5	6	7	8	9	10	11	12	13	14	15	16
Attack — vowel purity	15															
Breath control — humming	10															
Agility — range	15															
Legato — lower resonance	10															
Super breathing — posture	5															

Decide on the aspects of your singing which need the most work, combine two of them and make up an exercise for that combination. Divide your available time equally or proportionately and fill in the day's square when you've completed the work.

This is much simpler than the first chart, but it is effective. You can choose *only* those technical points which need the most work and you can practise for as little as five to ten minutes on each combination. By the way, don't *completely* neglect any detail of your technique, even if that area of your singing is good. Pay less attention to it in your practice periods if you wish, but give it an occasional airing to maintain its condition.

Using either of these schedules requires the singer to look up or make up some suitable exercises. In case you would like some help in devising these exercise-periods, or if you would like a sample thirty-minute practice schedule, here is an example:

Thirty-Minute Work-Out

WARM-UP, 5 mins.
    Along the lines mentioned earlier.

RESONANCE, 5 mins.
    Higher: hum throughout your voice on M, N, NG and HM, hum and opening

the lips to make a vowel sound, follow this exercise, use various vowels and various keys —

HM ___ I ___

Lower: practise opening the throat and dropping the jaw — create a huge space and keeping that wide open, yawning position, sing this phrase at a low pitch — sing all the vowels —

A ___

BREATHING, 5 mins.

Practise deep breathing out-of-doors with maximum breath intake and maximum emptying lungs. Alternate every other day with the sitting-down expansion exercise, lying-down deep breathing and holding a heavy object above your head.

Take a few very quick snatch-breaths.

Breath control — sing a note or a phrase with slow, steady outflow of breath, support the sound by pulling in tummy muscles, time yourself — thirty seconds is very good.

Sing messa di voce, very slowly — R.T.F. (repeat 'till fade), this is what it looks like again —

ATTACK AND ENDING THE NOTE, 5 mins.

Aim for a gentle, relaxed start to the note, feel the 'click', think about the pitch, the tongue and jaw positions — use a simple exercise containing all the vowels like this one —

I   E   A   O   U   Ü   ER   Á

Practise this ending the sound or phrasing-off exercise — each pair of notes is a phrase-end, taper-off the second note neatly — downwards and upward, try different vowels, different pitches and break at the commas.

Slow

ARTICULATION, 5 mins.

Vowel purity — speak the eight vowels, touch your throat, feel the different positions and mouth shapes — pure, distinct vowel sounds — now sing them on a low note, middle note and high note.

Diphthong combinations — use all the different combinations, make sure each vowel sound is right — here's one phrase —

I___E___A_____I___E___A_____I___E___A_____I___E___A_____I___E___A_

Consonants — aim for smart diction and L, M, N, R and Z in pitch. Read aloud a few sentences concentrating on clear, deliberate diction. Sing this exercise at various pitches and increasing speeds —

L   ost   M   ate   N   ine   R   ead   Z   oo

Legato — sing this exercise (or any tune you like) very smoothly, keep up the breath pressure, sing a phrase — not isolated notes. Aim for the last note. Sing different vowels and try different keys —

A ───►

AGILITY, 5 mins.

Practise this exercise for runs. With a light touch, accent the first note of each group, and try various speeds, vowels and keys —

This one is for range and clean arpeggios —

and this one is for ornaments and flexibility, sing it at increasing speeds —

That's a fairly comprehensive schedule and I guarantee you'll be sounding better even after a fortnight of doing it carefully — and *daily*. If you can do it twice a day — better still.

In addition to this well-balanced schedule, do as much as you like of the following:

Humming.

Relaxing and opening the throat space.

Breathing exercises out-of-doors.

Breath control exercises over a measured number of walking steps.

Sight reading practice.

Any exercises for the abdominal muscles — sit-ups, swimming, bicycling etc.

Sustained, quiet singing or humming on a fairly high note — one about five notes from your highest. (It helps in controlling a high-lying phrase sometimes known as a high *tessitura*.)

Listening to a wide variety of music — vocal and instrumental.

Improvement Record

When your singing is improving, you will hear it and feel it. If you would like to see the progress you can make charts or graphs to record your performance.

Graphs are fairly easy to devise — here are a couple of suggestions. One is for breath:

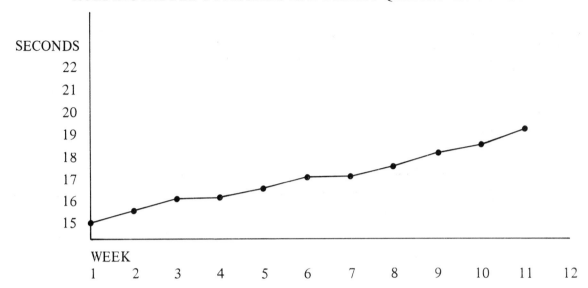

and one for agility:

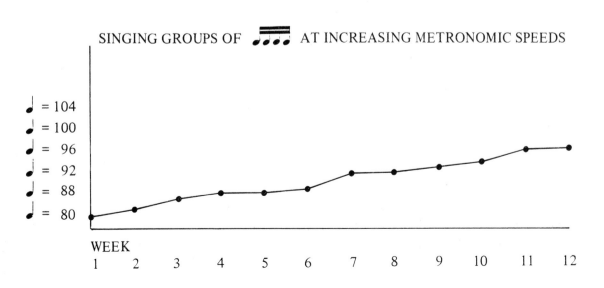

Here are two pages of music paper and two blank pages for your own exercises and charts.

NOTES AND CHARTS

CHAPTER EIGHT

VOCAL FAULTS: BAD HABITS AND HOW TO BREAK THEM

The 'natural' voice, that is to say one which has always been technically perfect in every respect, is so rare that we can almost forget that it exists. Most of us are born without vocal defects, but over the years, various influences (including 'nerves', our language, our personalities and habits) cause us to develop certain unfortunate faults which we are not aware of until either a teacher points them out or we hear ourselves singing on tape. Most of the faults are caused by poor techniques of breath control, attack and resonance so, if you perfect these three you shouldn't have many problems. And if you do have problems, don't worry — you're in good company. Every singer I know, including myself, has or has had trouble with his technique at one time or another.

Ask the opinion of someone you respect and criticise your singing on tape. Then, if you are not happy about something, the reason is probably here and the information will help you to work out the problem.

Fault No. 1 — 'Woolly' or 'Breathy' sound

It's difficult to describe the sound, but I think you will know what I mean. It's a sort of 'hoot', too much breath is escaping and not producing much voice. It has been heard from choir-boys and old ladies in the chorus!

All wind, but not much sound, the voice lacks a 'focus', a 'core', an 'edge' of sound.

It is caused by too much breath escaping through the vocal cords or not enough breath support — or both of these. If the vocal cords are not close enough together some air will escape without being 'used' — wasted air. Or if the pressure of the column of air from the lungs to the cords isn't being supported and reinforced by the diaphragm, the air pressure inside the lungs will fall and produce a 'vacuum', almost, which cannot make a strong sound.

The cure, of course, is to correct the start of the note and to develop a good breath support.

The attack is explained earlier on, but here is another exercise to help —

Simple exercises like this, done properly, will correct a breathy tone. I is perhaps the best vowel because it puts some tension in the vocal cords — but don't sing HI.

Take your time, concentrate on the attack, feel the 'click' which starts the note and you should make a clean sound. Be gentle at first, using the minimum amount of breath and try to make the sound 'within yourself'.

Try the other vowels, keeping some of the tension which I gives to the sound.

As far as breath control is concerned: the lowered air-pressure inside the lungs, which can make the weak 'woolly' sound, has to be replaced by a steady continuous pressure from pulling-in the tummy muscles to assist the diaphragm's support under the lungs. These two points can transform the sound of your voice.

Fault No. 2 — Dull, lifeless, colourless voice

This is fairly straightforward. It is caused by not using the resonance which is available. The sound you make is made mostly by the 'echo-chambers' of the throat, mouth and nasal space. The more you use them to develop resonance, the brighter, stronger your sound will become. The cure is to work on Chapter Five.

Fault No. 3 — 'Throaty' sound

Sometimes called guttural sound or 'swallowing the sound'. It's a constricted noise caused by the tongue choking the throat space and it is fairly common amongst 'Sergeant-Major' type bass singers in church choirs and choral societies. It is also found in wild pop music.

Why it is so easy to get into the habit of making a throaty sound, I don't know. But it is just as easy to correct it. The cure is to train the tongue to lie flat, out of the way, forward in the mouth away from the throat. In that position you can then 'yawn-open' the throat comfortably to produce a free unconstricted sound.

Here's a good exercise for training the tongue — and I've chosen an ascending phrase because going up a scale towards the top notes causes more tongue-trouble than lower notes:

A ————————————————————————————————————➤

Sing it wrongly first, to remind you what the trouble is. Let the tongue move up and back and notice the hollow, strained, throaty noise you make. Then deliberately open the throat, keep the tip of your tongue against the back of the teeth, creating a lot of space, and sing it again. The sound will be free, vibrant, and you will feel relaxed and comfortable. That is the sound you must train yourself to expect. With a bit of practice, you will get into the habit of feeling your tongue position and you will become accustomed to making this free, unrestricted sound.

Fairly easy really — just a matter of training. At first, sing the exercise in a comfortable key on the easier vowels — A and E. Then try the more closed sounds.

When you are happy with the sound in the middle of your voice — and not before — transpose the phrase up a semitone at a time until your highest notes are reached.

Here are the first two transpositions — I'll leave the others to you.

Fault No. 4 — Vowel Troubles

Dull, indistinct vowel sounds are fairly common. It's very easy, almost 'natural' to get into the habit.

Dull, flat, lifeless vowel 'colours', lacking in brilliance — I think you know the sound and it can be heard from non-Latin singers in particular. The reason, I think, is that our language lacks 'brightness' and 'colour' — and we naturally sing as we speak. However, lifeless sounds have no place in singing, so we must try to brighten them up in any way we can.

For most people, the vowels E, A and U are the dullest, and I the brightest. If you work from the brightest sound and add some of its brilliance into the other vowels, you can develop consistently bright sounds. Here's a useful exercise to help you —

I _____ E _____ A _____

Get a bright sound, keep it high and bright—especially   HERE . . . .

Choose your brightest vowel (it's probably I) and sing this exercise in your middle/upper range. Make a brilliant sound on the first vowel and when changing to E, *will* it to stay brilliant, don't let the sound 'drop into the mouth' — plenty of 'air' in E, and concentrate even more when you change to A.

Make up your own exercises for the other vowels and get into the habit of thinking like this.

The other common vowel trouble is impure, indistinct vowel sounds. The next time you watch singing on TV — any style of singing — look closely at the people's faces and listen to their sounds critically.

Church congregations are very good value for this and cameramen often oblige by focussing on the most comical faces! And it's the tight, stiff-upper-lip, immobile faces which produce the words you can't understand.

Vowels, consonants and words are difficult enough to understand in most people's *speech*, but they have no chance of getting across all that space, orchestra and rhythm unless they are *deliberately exaggerated*.

I is, or should be, clearly different from Ü, A from Á, O from U, E from ER — and all should be different from each other. And to make them so, you have to spend time working on the larynx area which makes the vowels and the mouth, lips and tongue which perfect them.

Pop music singers — one more point for you especially — please don't sing LERVE for LOVE!

Here's an exercise for you to think about —

The different sounds are made by the vocal cords — as you can observe if you put your finger between your teeth and sing them. But they can become even more distinct if you use your throat, mouth space and lips to refine them. It needs mobility and, when singing in public, it needs deliberate shaping for each vowel.

If you are self-conscious, you'll have to develop some abandon to exaggerate like this. But it will do good things to your singing (I guarantee you will be complimented on your diction) — and to your speech!

Fault No. 5 — Gear-Changing

I once heard Jackie Stewart say that the secret of Grand-Prix driving is the smoothness and precision of gear changing. This could also be said of singing, and the gears in the voice are the 'registers' or areas from which the voice seems to originate. High notes, particularly in high voices, seem to be made in the head and have a light, ringing sound. The lowest notes, especially in low voices, have a thick, dark quality which seems to be made in the throat and chest. And middle notes are felt and have a quality somewhere in between these extremes.

The fault is that, in singing a wide-ranging phrase, these different qualities can easily, in the untrained singer, sound like different 'voices' — different singers almost. This breaks up a phrase, makes it inconsistent and, I think, ugly.

It can be cured by developing enough skill to control your use of resonance, carrying the heavy chest sound up to the higher notes, and carrying the brighter 'head voice' resonance down to the lower notes.

In a descending phrase, the danger-point is about five notes from your lowest, where a 'break' occurs and the chest voice begins. Work around that point, trying to smooth-out the gear-change by coaxing the high resonance down and the chest resonance up.

Fault No. 6 — Forcing or Overblowing

There is a strong temptation, especially in men, to make a bigger sound than they are equipped to make. It happens a lot in dramatic music, on high notes and when you are trying to hear yourself against the loud instrumental sound around you — whether it's amplified pop music or sweeping orchestral music.

This forcing or 'overblowing' produces a harsh, uncontrolled sound and it can permanently damage the delicate vocal cords. Programme your mind with the fact that there is a limit to the number of decibels your vocal apparatus can produce. Not even the biggest voices can compete with amplified music, a concert organ, forty other voices or the fat brass section of a symphony orchestra.

The only way your voice can sound loud is by developing from correct quiet singing, using maximum resonating space and maximum breath pressure and support. And there is a limit on that. Perfect your technique of quiet singing — making the sound 'within yourself' and not 'pushing it outwards'. Then you can build up the resonance and the breath pressure to the extent of *your* potential, and no further.

Fault No. 7 — Intonation Problems

This isn't an easy one to cure. It is singing out of tune and the problems are that the singer often isn't aware of it and that it can take a long time to correct.

The pitch of your notes is helped by a well-developed upper resonance, but resonance alone cannot correct bad intonation. I think the main cause of singing out of tune is an under-developed pitch sense — a poor musical ear. My advice is to develop a sense of precise pitch — listen to the intonation of other singers — criticise your own singing. Play a chord on any well-tuned instrument, listen hard to the pitch of the notes, hear the exact pitch of any note in your 'mind's ear' before singing it, carry a tuning-fork around, record yourself singing unaccompanied and check the pitch on a piano — and so on. Gradually you will develop an acute sense of pitch and cure the fault.

Fault No. 8 — Wobble, Excess Vibrato

When string-players shake their left hands quickly they are producing vibrato — tiny, almost unnoticeable alterations in the pitch of a note to give it a 'warmth'.

Vibrato also occurs, naturally, in singing.

Excessive and uncontrolled vibrato makes an unsteady 'shaky' sound which we can call wobble. (Not tremolo, which is a feature of the instrumentalist's technique and means something different.) It is caused by poor breathing and breath control — not enough breath being inhaled and a lack of strong muscular support of the air-pressure in the lungs.

A few weeks' work on Chapters One and Two is the cure, and to start you off here are a few useful exercises.

Hum

Take a good breath, hum on a fairly high note, keep the same volume — steady, no wobbling! — and sustain it for twenty or more seconds. This will encourage your muscles of support to work. When you can control the steadiness of the hum, go on to vowel sounds —

Slow, steady, quiet

I_____ E_____ A_____ O_____ U_____ Ü_____ ER_____ A_____

Again keep the volume steady and quiet throughout — be aware of the work your tummy muscles have to do to support the sound. Then 'play' with your control in the messa di voce —

As slow as you like

A <——> O <——> U <——>

Gradual, steady, controlled — keep the note in tune — don't wobble!

Fault No. 9 — Breathing in the Wrong Place

There's only one place to break your singing for a breath, and that's the right place — determined by the punctuation, the sense of the words and the music. Just as in speaking.

In the same way that words are grouped in phrases, and for a similar reason, music is written in phrases. Lyricists punctuate the flow of words, good composers write accordingly and singers should respect their phrasing.

The principal cause of breathing in the wrong place is running out of breath — an understandable excuse, but, unfortunately, not acceptable to the discriminating ear of the musical director, the producer or the person who pays money to hear you sing.

For all____ we know____ we may ne - ver meet a - gain____

There's only one place to breathe in this phrase, isn't there? After 'again' — although I've heard the phrase broken after 'know'.

Think of all phrases being played by an organ or a violin — they don't break because they don't have breathing problems — neither should the singer.

Fault No. 10 — Diphthongs or Vowel Mixing

We talked earlier on about words like 'mind', 'here' and 'open', which contain diphthongs or vowel mixtures. The word 'round', for instance, has the mixture of A and U, — RA-U-ND. In speech we get over the words so quickly that the diphthongs are hardly noticed, but in singing, sustaining the sound makes it necessary to give some thought to the exact positioning of the second vowel of every diphthong. Here is a classic example —

I'll get by ____ as long as I ____ have you ____

The points which need some thought are 'by' and 'I'. Have you ever noticed this sort of thing:

BA __ I __   A __ I __

'I'll get byEE as long as I-EE have you'. She definitely wouldn't have me if she sang like that! Have you every heard that? It's fairly common in show-biz type singing, and it's the *ultimate* turn-off for me.

If you think about diphthongs and sing a few examples, I think you'll agree that a better position for the second vowel is *just before the end of the note*, i.e. the shorter the better. Something like this —

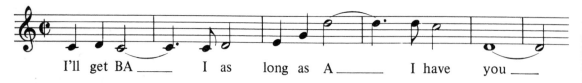

I'll get BA ____ I as long as A ____ I have you ____

As you can see, most of the troubles you are likely to come across are caused by wrong technique of breath control, starting the note, and resonance. If you can put these three right, your singing will improve by the day. But your singing cannot get better if one or more of these fundamental aspects isn't right.

I strongly advise you to work carefully on the first five chapters.

CHAPTER NINE

READING MUSIC

Whatever type of singing you do, you'll do it more easily if you can read music. And the preceding pages have assumed some basic understanding of musical notation. This chapter is for those who experience a sense of helplessness when looking at printed music and not having the faintest idea what's going on.

A page of music to one person is about as meaningful as *The Times* crossword in hieroglyphics, but to another it's *music* which he can 'hear'. Highly trained musicians can 'read' and understand printed music almost as well as they can read a newspaper. And that means being able to 'hear' (or imagine) a performance of it! Every singer who isn't completely tone deaf can develop some of that ability with training. It isn't easy — because you have to learn another language — but you *can* learn to read music even if you don't have a special musical talent. All those black dots and squiggles and things are the alphabet of music and you have to learn what they mean. For singing at sight, you have to sing the right notes at the right time.

Singing the Right Notes

The immensely complicated business of translating musical ideas into black and white has, over the centuries, been solved by a system of which the principal feature for us, at the moment, is the scale. The scale is the line of notes doh, ray, me, fah, soh, lah, te, doh — seven different notes and an eighth which is the same as the first but at a higher pitch. And those seven different notes are the seven letters from which musical 'words' and phrases are made. They are the basic ingredients of tunes, and from them we can make thousands of different tunes. (There are a few more notes, but we'll come to those later.)

If there is a piano handy, play a long line of white notes. Your ear will tell you where the scale starts, and you will notice that the scale repeats itself a few times until you run out of notes and fall off the stool!

Those are the notes which the composer has at his disposal and this is how he writes those notes on paper —

He writes them on two sets of five lines. (A few hundred years ago he used eleven lines. But since that was a bit confusing for the eye, two sets of five replaced eleven — and a small middle line is drawn in by the composer when he needs it.)

The seven notes of the scale are christened with a letter-name. So are these lines and that's the system we use. The letter-names are A B C D E F G, and they are these white notes on a piano —

repeated from the bottom to the top.

The corresponding names of the lines and spaces are —

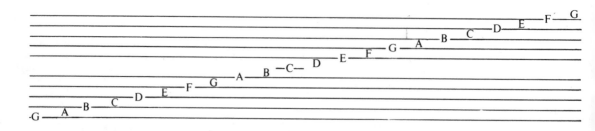

The note-span of all the voices is about four consecutive scales. That's about twenty-eight white notes in the middle of a piano.

This diagram shows that span and how the composer indicates the notes on the eleven lines.

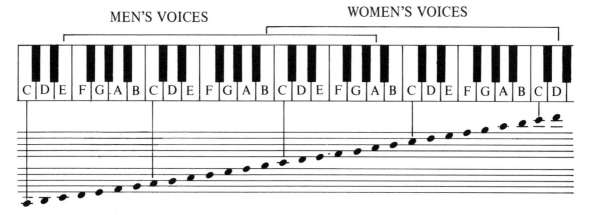

The higher notes are written on the upper five lines (or 'stave') and the men's notes on the lower stave. The composer indicates which pitch he wants by writing the Treble Clef (𝄞) or the Bass Clef (𝄢) at the beginning of each.

You now know about the names of the notes and how they look on paper. But how does that help you to sing printed music when there isn't a piano about?

It doesn't. To sing the right notes you also need to know a bit more about scales and something about intervals — the distance between notes.

Lets go back to that doh, ray, me, scale — it is a major scale and, on paper, it looks like this —

And in the Bass
Clef at a lower pitch

That's a major scale, C D E F G A B C — and I've linked the two important positions where semitones occur, i.e. between E and F and between B and C. All the other distances are whole-tones and so a major scale is made up of — tone, tone, semitone, tone, tone, tone, semitone. That's important. The order of tones and semitones determines the sound of a scale.

I'll repeat that — a major scale is made up of seven intervals —

tone, tone, ½-tone, tone, tone, tone, ½-tone

That's the major scale then — the seven different notes from which thousands of tunes can be made. Here's one of those tunes — it's a National Anthem which is occasionally heard at the Olympic Games —

It is written using those seven notes of the scale — those seven white notes on a piano—C D E F G A B. We say it is written in the scale of C major or the 'key' of C major.

If you try to sing this tune starting on the note C you'll probably think its a bit low. You might prefer to sing it a bit higher — say starting on G.

Here is the scale written out starting on G — the major scale starting on G — but don't forget that order of tones and semitones.

These are the notes of a scale starting on G — G A B C D E F G and I've marked the semitones. The semitones aren't right, are they? The first one is, but the second should be between the seventh and eighth notes. When you re-write a scale at a different pitch *the order of tones and semitones has to be preserved*. To keep the order correct we have to use the black notes, in this case F sharp, and the scale becomes G A B C D E F sharp G. The order of tones and semitones is right and it sounds like a major scale.

Using these notes we can write the National Anthem at a more comfortable pitch —

That is in the key of G major — the scale which has one sharp. Suppose you want to write it starting on D?

This is the major scale starting on D — with the correct order of tones and semitones preserved —

D E F G A B C♯ D

And here is that well-known tune in the key of D —

We don't have to write a sharp sign (♯) before every F and C. We can, and do, write those two sharps on the stave at the beginning of a piece and that indicates that all F's and C's in the tune are always sung as F♯s and C♯s. Like this:  It's called a 'key-signature' — and the example on the previous page should properly be written like this —

without the need to write a ♯ before every C and F in the music.

The same tune starting on F would also need a black note — B flat. It's the same note as A♯ but in the key of F major we already have an A natural. A♯ would be more trouble to write, so we call the black note B flat.

The scale of F looks like this:

and the National Anthem in the key of F major looks like this —

If a composer wanted to start this tune, or any tune, on B, E♭, A♭ or F♯ he would have to use other keys and more black notes — more sharps and flats. There are several different major keys: seven using sharps and seven using flats apart from C major which doesn't have sharps or flats.

Here are all the major scales or keys, with their semitones marked and with their key signatures.

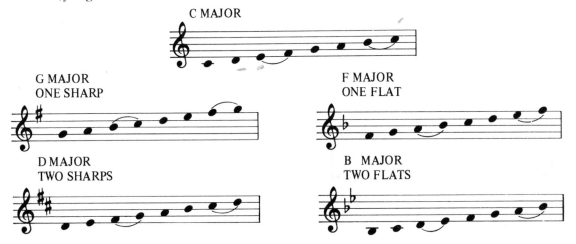

Minor Scales and Keys

Because words and music express a variety of emotions and not only noise, composers need the ability to transmit their feeling through the sounds at their disposal. The major scales sound 'bright' and 'cheerful', but a different order of tones and semitones can change the scale's 'atmosphere' to a feeling of sadness or 'darkness'.

The scale of C major, for instance,

sounds contented enough. But if you change a few notes

it gets the blues.

This new 'feel' is caused entirely by changing the order of tones and semitones. The third, sixth and seventh notes are a semitone lower than in the C major scale — and this new order makes up a minor scale — in this case C minor. Just three notes changed and the effect is completely different.

In fact, the sixth and seventh notes aren't that important — they can both be flats, both naturals or one of each and the atmosphere is still the same. What is important, though, is the third note. That has to be a semitone lower than its major brother.

The flat third — *the 'blue' note* — the demon who delivers those fatal arrows!

The minor scale, then, transmits the composer's less-happy feelings and it does so principally as a result of the lowered third note.

'Scarborough Fair', which we mentioned in another chapter is an example of a not-so-happy song written in a minor key — E minor.

Are you go - ing____ to Scar - bo-rough Fair

The deadly lowered third is G — not G sharp — but G natural. Had this tune been written in a major key, G sharp would have been used — completely changing the mood.

The minor scale, then, has a lowered third note — but it also has a sixth note and a seventh note which may be flat, natural or sharp as the composer wishes.

That's A minor — the minor scale which is related to C major by virtue of the fact that neither uses sharps or flats in the key signature, and the all-important semitone position is marked.

As with the major scale, you can transpose minor keys to different pitches — so long as you preserve the order of semitones. Here are the other minor scales, with their key signatures and their 'blue' thirds marked.

E MINOR
ONE SHARP

D MINOR
ONE FLAT

B MINOR
TWO SHARPS

G MINOR
TWO FLATS

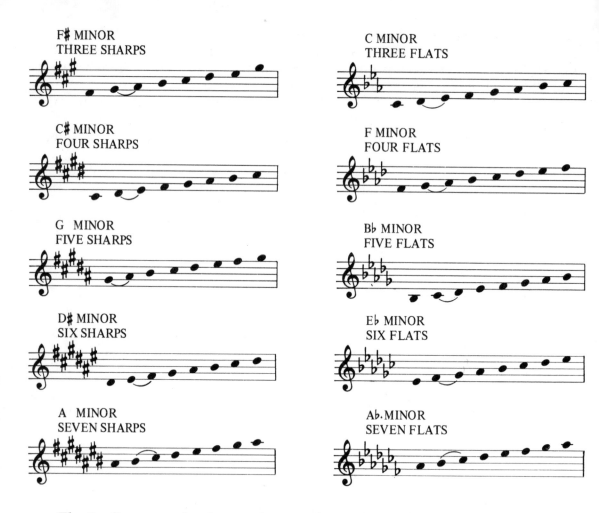

F# MINOR
THREE SHARPS

C MINOR
THREE FLATS

C# MINOR
FOUR SHARPS

F MINOR
FOUR FLATS

G MINOR
FIVE SHARPS

Bb MINOR
FIVE FLATS

D# MINOR
SIX SHARPS

Eb MINOR
SIX FLATS

A MINOR
SEVEN SHARPS

Ab MINOR
SEVEN FLATS

That's all you need to know about scales and keys for the time being. I know it's confusing at first, but, in time, it will 'click' and the information so far will help you enormously in singing-at-sight.

If you have time, write out some scales, get to know what they look like and memorize them. It's vital to know how sounds look on paper.

Intervals

Singing the right notes at sight means singing accurately, whatever notes are printed.

Suppose you see an F♯ followed by a D, followed by an E —

how do you know which notes to sing — how do you know the right pitch? There are a few people who have a sense of 'absolute pitch', or 'perfect pitch'. These people can give you any note you ask for within a split second. They have this remarkable ability of knowing *precisely* the pitch of any note, whatever they are doing, any time of the day or night. For these rare people, pitch is no problem — they can sing notes as accurately as a pianist can play them. The rest of us can't be sure what F♯ sounds like until we hear it on an instrument or a tuning fork. But we can work out what F♯ sounds like *in relation to D*. If you know that the above three notes are the third, top and second notes of a major scale, then *imagine* how they sound, you can sing them. It is possible to 'hear' what any note sounds like in relation to any other — and that is called having a sense of 'relative pitch'.

If you know that these notes are the fifth, third, second and first notes of a minor scale and you are familiar with the sounds of a minor scale, you can *imagine* them and sing them. It's fairly straightforward then — you have to be able to imagine or 'hear' in your mind any interval in those scales.

Something else which helps is knowing the names of all intervals. If you know that D up to B♭ is a minor sixth interval, for instance, and you know how a minor sixth sounds, you can sing the notes. Now, intervals are named according to how many *names* of notes they span — inclusively.

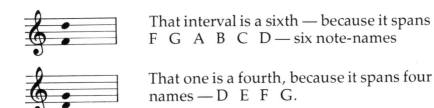

That interval is a sixth — because it spans
F G A B C D — six note-names

That one is a fourth, because it spans four
names — D E F G.

That's the rule — an interval is named according to how many note-names it spans. The intervals in a major scale are named like this —

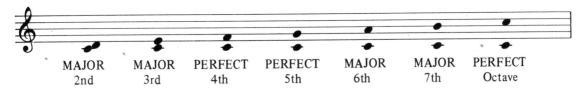

| MAJOR 2nd | MAJOR 3rd | PERFECT 4th | PERFECT 5th | MAJOR 6th | MAJOR 7th | PERFECT Octave |

Every major scale has the same interval names. In E♭ they look like this —

| MAJOR 2nd | MAJOR 3rd | PERFECT 4th | PERFECT 5th | MAJOR 6th | MAJOR 7th | PERFECT Octave |

In minor keys, as you know, the third, sixth and seventh notes are different — so here's how we name the intervals in minor scales — all of them.

C MINOR

MAJOR	MINOR	PERFECT	PERFECT	MINOR	MINOR	PERFECT
2nd	3rd	4th	5th	6th	7th	Octave

As you might have guessed, the third, sixth and seventh notes make different intervals from their major equivalents, so they are called minor intervals. That's the system of naming intervals.

How are you doing so far? Are you beginning to have noises in the head yet? Have a go at imagining a major third — and then a perfect fifth.

Can you see how you can work out what any two notes sound like in relation to each other? I'm sure you can — and I'm sure you are beginning to think of a phrase such as this —

in terms of a major sixth, a major third, a perfect fourth followed by a perfect fifth.

So far, we have talked about the intervals which are made up of the first notes and another note from the major and minor scales. And the vast majority of intervals you come across will fall into this category. Except little horrors like these:

There are a few awkward intervals like these, but, mercifully, we don't often have to sing them. However, as we do occasionally find them, we have to know their names and what they sound like. They are called DIMINISHED and AUGMENTED intervals. A diminished interval is an interval which is one semitone less than a minor interval or a perfect interval. An augmented interval is an interval which is one semitone more than a major interval or a perfect interval.

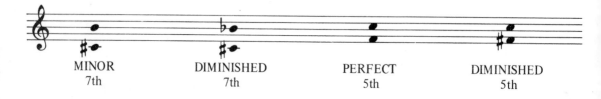

MINOR	DIMINISHED	PERFECT	DIMINISHED
7th	7th	5th	5th

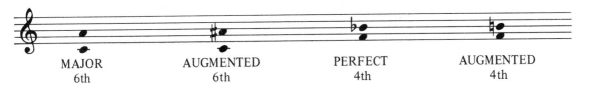

MAJOR	AUGMENTED	PERFECT	AUGMENTED
6th	6th	4th	4th

That, very briefly, is all you need to know about intervals in order to sing the right notes. If this information is new to you, the odds are that you find it mind-boggling. Don't worry — carry the book about and take in a bit at a time. Within a few weeks you'll begin to see the light.

Singing the Notes at the Right Time

Assuming you can sing the right notes, all you need to do now is sing them at the right time — then you can read music perfectly. You need to learn about note lengths and rests — the tempo or pace at which the notes travel — in a word, rhythm.

Not the *pitch* of a note, but its *'beat'*. Whether regular, like your heartbeat and the tick of a clock, or irregular like the rap of Morse code and birdsong.

If we had to indicate a regulat beat in a diagram, we might do something like —

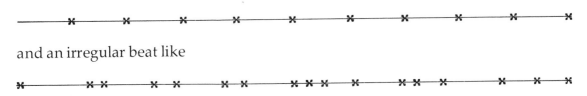

and an irregular beat like

A composer has to tell the singers how long the notes should last and he indicates the length of a note by its *shape*.

Here are some notes: ♩ ♩ ♪ ○ ♪ — they are all different shapes so they all last different lengths of time.

This table shows the notes we use, indicating their length in relation to each other. Each is half as long as the next.

The semiquaver

The quaver

The crotchet

The minim

The semibreve

In America they are called by descriptive names —

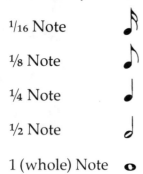

¹/₁₆ Note

¹/₈ Note

¹/₄ Note

¹/₂ Note

1 (whole) Note

Imagine the rhythm of your heartbeat — count it or clap it —

It's a steady beat — the time between each beat is the same, the length of each beat is the same. We can show that rhythm with notes — seven notes of the same length. Let's choose the crotchet —

1   2   3   4   5   6   7

That's the crotchet beat. The quaver beat would be twice as fast. Tap it —

1   2   3   4   5   6   7

The semiquaver beat, four times as fast. Four quick taps to each heartbeat —

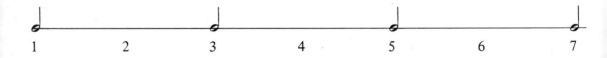

1   2   3   4   5   6   7

The minim beat would be half as fast. A slow note. Tap slowly —

1   2   3   4   5   6   7

84

And the semibreve, slower still. Have a go at that —

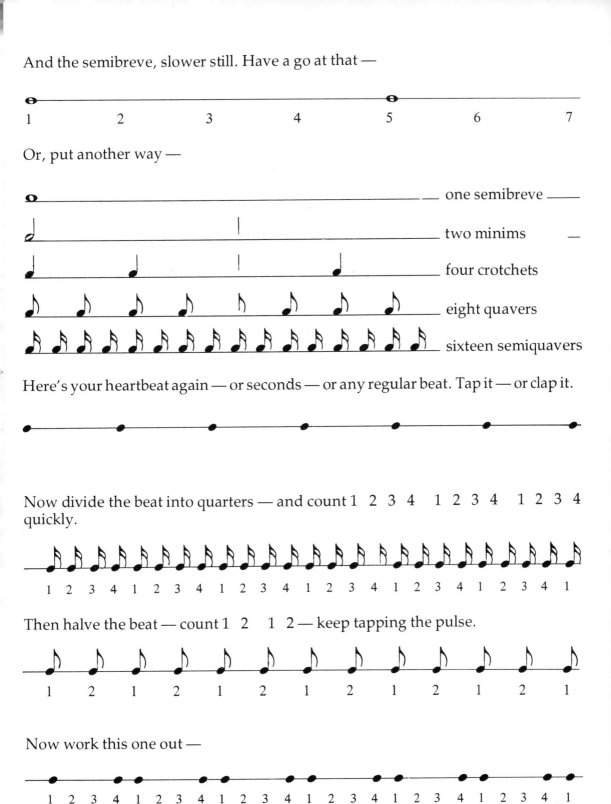

Or, put another way —

one semibreve

two minims

four crotchets

eight quavers

sixteen semiquavers

Here's your heartbeat again — or seconds — or any regular beat. Tap it — or clap it.

Now divide the beat into quarters — and count 1 2 3 4   1 2 3 4   1 2 3 4 quickly.

1 2 3 4 1 2 3 4 1 2 3 4 1 2 3 4 1 2 3 4 1 2 3 4 1

Then halve the beat — count 1 2   1 2 — keep tapping the pulse.

1   2   1   2   1   2   1   2   1   2   1   2   1

Now work this one out —

1 2 3 4 1 2 3 4 1 2 3 4 1 2 3 4 1 2 3 4 1 2 3 4 1

The first note lasts three-quarters of a beat and the short one is a quarter. You must have heard that rhythm — perhaps on a train journey. The way the composer indicates that uneven rhythm is like this —

With a dot after a note.
The dot lengthens a note by half. So ♪. = (♪ + ♪), (♪ + ♪) = 4 ♪ or 1 ♩ As in the American National Anthem.

1   2   3   4

A dot after a note adds half to its length.

$$\mathbf{o}\cdot = (\mathbf{o} \; + \; \mathbf{\mathit{d}})$$

$$\mathbf{\mathit{d}}\cdot = (\mathbf{\mathit{d}} \; + \; \mathbf{\mathit{d}})$$

$$\mathbf{\mathit{d}}\cdot = (\mathbf{\mathit{d}} \; + \; \mathbf{\mathit{d}\mathit{)})$$

$$\mathbf{\mathit{d}}\cdot = (\mathbf{\mathit{d}} \; + \; \mathbf{\mathit{d}\mathit{)})$$

Another way of lengthening a note is by tying it to another with this mark ⌣ . It means 'plus', i.e.   ♩ ⌣ ♩ = ♩ + ♩

$$\mathbf{o}\cdot = \mathbf{o} \underline{} \mathbf{\mathit{d}}$$

$$\mathbf{\mathit{d}}\cdot = \mathbf{\mathit{d}} \underline{} \mathbf{\mathit{d}}$$

$$\mathbf{\mathit{d}}\cdot = \mathbf{\mathit{d}} \underline{} \mathbf{\mathit{d}}$$

$$\mathbf{\mathit{d}}\cdot = \mathbf{\mathit{d}} \underline{} \mathbf{\mathit{d}}$$

That would *sound* the same as the previous example.
   If it's driving you insane, stop now and come back to it tomorrow. It's the sort of thing which is very difficult to put into words but which is second nature once

you 'feel' it. Like driving a car. Take it a section at a time, slowly, and get somebody else to read it with you. It will all fall into place in time.

If it isn't driving you insane, let's go on.

Back to your heartbeat —

You know how to write four notes to the beat, and two. What about three — or five? Try to count three between each tap —

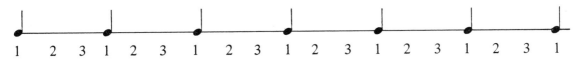

1   2   3   1   2   3   1   2   3   1   2   3   1   2   3   1   2   3   1

Every count is a third of a crotchet — there isn't such a note! So we indicate 'triplets' like this —

Three notes in the time of one crotchet.

Three notes in the time of one quaver would look like this —

And three notes in the time of one minim, like this —

Groups of five are written in a similar way —

Those are the note lengths, then. They don't have to last any particular number of seconds. They don't have *actual* length. They have *relative* length — in relation to other notes.

There is rhythm or beat everywhere. Seasons, cycles, ebb and flow, rise and fall. Action and rest, day and night, noise and quiet, excitement and calm, strong and weak. Various patterns which make things interesting — and without which life, and music would be monotonous.

Music isn't churned out of a sausage machine: it's a spontaneous reaction to life — and to 'feeling', especially vocal music with its additional message of words. It has natural rhythm, natural up and down, some fast some slow, some strong beats, some not-so-strong. It's impossible to imagine otherwise.

Think about the rhythm of a waltz — or the American National Anthem. You can 'feel' **1** 2 3 in either, can't you? 1 is stronger than 2 and 3. Think about soldiers marching, or almost any rock music — that's in four, **1** 2 3 4, **1** 2 3 4 — the first beat stronger than the others. All music is like that — sometimes with a 2 'feel', sometimes 6 — (**1** 2 3 4 5 6), occasionally 5.

Composers tell you what rhythm they have in mind — not that they need to do so because you can feel it — by writing a 'time signature' after the key signature. Like these —

The top number tells you how many beats there are in the 'feel' (*not all strong*), and the bottom number tells you which length of beat —

4 means quarter note — (or crotchet — ♩)

8 means eighth note — (or quaver — ♪)

16 means sixteenth note — (or semiquaver — ♬)

2 means half note — (or minim — ♩)

Composers also indicate the rhythm by dividing up the notes into 'groups of rhythm' with vertical bar lines —

Again, these lines aren't absolutely essential, as you can 'feel' the rhythm — but they do make a line of notes easier on your eye. However, they have the disadvantage of breaking up long phrases into small bits or 'bars' — so, for that reason, I hope you don't waste a lot of time worrying about bar lines.

Finally, we have to learn about rests — the symbols which indicate silence. They're easy.

The note	o	𝅗𝅥	♩	♪	♪
Its rest	▬	▬	· 𝄽 or 𝄾	𝄾	𝄿

For a whole bar's rest we use the semibreve rest, irrespective of how long the bar is, and the rare dotted rest corresponds with a dotted note.

That, in brief, is some of the data with which you must be programmed to read and understand music. Notice I say *in brief*, because, although there is enough information here to help you learn to read, it's only a fraction of the total language of music.

CODA

We have now covered almost all the areas any singer needs to know about to perfect his technique. Most of the practical side of singing has been explained in sufficient detail to give you safe and helpful guidance for years of training and application. If you work on what we've talked about, your singing is bound to improve — your friends will notice the improvement and you will hear the difference yourself.

Good singing, though, is not made up *only* of isolated aspects of practical vocal technique. A singer isn't a computer consisting of dozens of perfectly manufactured components — he must be principally a creative artist, or, at least, an interpreter of someone else's creativity. You have to be a performer as well as a machine and so you need other skills in addition to perfectly working bits and pieces. These include general musicianship, interpretation, repertoire, foreign languages, acting and presentation — and none of them can be covered in this short handbook.

I strongly encourage you to work on becoming well-equipped in these non-singing subjects, all of which should be absolutely essential to anyone who sings. Go and have lessons with qualified teachers and experienced singers if you can — there should be someone suitable in your district. And if there isn't, you will be able to find plenty of good books, if you look for them.

Here are some of the most important things you should get to know about.

General Musicianship

Rhythm, tempo, pitch, sightreading, phrasing, ear training, vocal blend (in groups) and harmony.

Interpretation

Getting the meaning of words and music across to the listener, transmitting your feelings, your interpretation of the music by variety, expression and word emphasis. In the case of early music, folk and traditional music, anything written before about 1800 (when composers didn't always indicate how they wanted the music to be performed) in fact, deciding how you think the composer might have preferred the tempo or the volume. And, as far as ornaments are concerned, becoming familiar with the singing customs of the time.

Even in modern music — how fast is 'fast', how slow is 'adagio', how many decibels in 'pp' and how far should you 'cresc.'? They are all relative — only you can decide, you are the interpreter.

Repertoire

1. Singers are always being asked, at short notice, to do a concert or a recording,

sometimes including new music, music they haven't looked at for ages and music which they have never seen.

2.   Most singers, at all stages of their lives, have to audition for promoters, conductors and agents — and if they mean business, they will have prepared a selection of suitable music in various styles which they are able to sing well.

3.   The music which is regularly performed is only the tip of the iceberg — there is a limitless amount of marvellous music which is never heard. Some of it is unpublished, out of print or difficult to get hold of — but it can be found.

Any one of these is good enough reason to form or re-form your repertoire now. It is never too early or too late to reassess your vocal potential, taking expert advice if you can.

So, write your own repertoire book — include everything you might be asked to sing, list items you would like to sing, learn the music and cover the repertoire's entire technical demands in your training sessions.

Foreign Languages

In so-called 'serious' or 'classical' music, the amount of vocal music written in English is small — the bulk of it is in Italian, Latin, German and French. Even in popular music there is a fair repertoire of songs in languages other than English.

In a perfect world, all singers would be fluent in the above five languages. All that most of us can manage, unfortunately, is a smattering of each. Make sure, though, that your smattering includes perfect pronunciation and verbal accentuation, an understanding of the meaning of the words you sing and, in theatrical music, knowing what the others are singing about.

Acting and Presentation

The way a singer presents himself, both on stage and to individuals, is the subject on which all the most effective performers and management spend time and money and it is also the most common factor in any singer's fulfilment or downfall. There's not much point in being a marvellous singer if no one ever asks you to sing because you're an embarrassment on and off stage!

There are a few natural charmers who seem to get away with incompetence and remain in demand — for a while, at least. You're not one of them — if you were, you wouldn't be reading this book. So I hope you encourage yourself to do something about the way others see you. Think about movement, gesture, positioning, your appearance, facial expression and your conversation — things which cannot be learned from a book. Established professional coaches and experience are the best teachers.

A MUSIC PHRASE-BOOK

Italian is still the international language of music, in spite of the introduction of English, German and French words in some composers' scores in recent years. Almost every piece of printed music you can buy has some instructions in the original Italian.

Here is a check-list of the more common terms a singer comes across and, although it isn't comprehensive, you can learn a useful working knowledge of the musical language from it.

Term	What it Means	Its Abbreviation
A CAPPELLA	Unaccompanied	
A TEMPO	At (the original) speed	
ACCELERANDO	Gradually getting quicker	ACCEL.
ADAGIO	Slowly	
ALLA	In the style of	
ALLARGANDO	Getting broader	
ALLEGRETTO	Not so fast as allegro, but nearly so	
ALLEGRO	Quickly	
ANDANTE	Flowing along — not fast, not slow	
ARIA	A long, and often elaborate, vocal solo in opera or oratorio	
ASSAI	Usually means very	
BEL CANTO	The classic style of seventeenth- and eighteenth-century Italian singing	
BOCCA CHIUSA	With the mouth closed — i.e. humming	
CALMATO	Calm	
CODA	A final section, usually a few bars to finish off a song	
COLLA VOCE	With the voice — for accompanists to follow the singer	
CON	With	

CON MOTO	With movement	
CRESCENDO	Getting louder gradually	cresc. or $<$
DA CAPO	Go back to the beginning	D.C.
DAL SEGNO	Repeat from this sign 𝄋	D.S.
DIMINUENDO	Gradually getting quieter	Dim.
FERMATA	Pause	𝄐
FINE	The end (of a song)	fin
FORTE	Loud	*f*
FORTISSIMO	Very loud	*ff*
GIOCOSO	Joyfully	
LEGATO	Smoothly — notes performed joined together	
LENTO	Slowly	
LUNGA	Long	
MARCATO	Marked — the note to be emphasised	
MENO MOSSO	Less moved — i.e. slower	
MESSA DI VOCE	Expressive crescendo and diminuendo on one note	$<>$
MEZZA VOCE	'Half-voice'	
MEZZO FORTE	Only moderately loud	*mf*
MEZZO PIANO	Only moderately quiet	*mp*
MODERATO	At a moderate speed	
MOLTO	Very	
NIENTE	Nothing — often means diminuendo until silent	
PAUSA	Rest	
PIANISSIMO	Very quiet	*pp*
PIANO	Quiet	*p*
PIU	More	
POCO	A little — i.e. rather	
POCO A POCO	Little by little	

PORTAMENTO	A slide between notes	
PRESTO	Quickly	
RALLENTANDO	Gradually slower	RALL.
RITARDANDO	Holding back — same as rallentando	RIT.
SEMPRE	Always	
SENZA	Without	
SIMILE	Similarly — continue in the foregoing style	
SOSTENUTO	Sustained	
STACCATO	Detached — opposite of legato, its symbol is a dot over a note	
SUBITO	Suddenly	
TACET	Silent — often means omit	
TUTTI	All or everyone	
UNISON	All voices singing the same tune — not in harmony	UNIS.
VIVACE	Vivacious	
VIVO	Lively	
VOLTI SUBITO	Turn over (the page!) quickly	V.S.